CONTENTS

Welcome 4
Declaration and Affirmation 5

INTRODUCTION

What is an elder? 7
The road to eldership 10
Discerning a call to eldership 12

FUNDAMENTALS

The authority of the creeds 16
Our foundational text: the Bible 18
Our foundational act: prayer 20
The Church and the advancement of the kingdom of God 21

UNDERSTANDING THE KIRK

An introduction to John Knox 27
What does it mean to be "Reformed"? 29
The Westminster Confession – past and present 31
The courts of the Kirk 34
What is a Kirk Session? 35
The spiritual office of the elder 36
An introduction to Church discipline 38
The elder and the minister 40

SERVING IN THE KIRK

The elder and public worship 43
Serving the sacraments 45
Creating communities of belonging 47
Kirk Sessions: listening and acting 50
Peace and unity of the Church 52
Pastoring the parish 58
Making hospital visits 60
Caring for the bereaved 62
How will our children have faith? 64
Discipleship 66
Missional thinking: a light to the nation 68
Elders and the environment 70
Ecumenical thinking: working with others 71

Central support 73

About this publication:
This is an educational resource for elders in the Church of Scotland. It is designed to generate discussion and should not be read as authoritative. Any conflict between this publication and Church law or civil law is unintentional, and this resource is entirely subordinate to the legislation and official documents of the General Assembly of the Church of Scotland.

WELCOME

Rt Rev John Chalmers
Moderator of the General Assembly of the Church of Scotland

> " **One of the strengths of this publication is that it draws on the great breadth and diversity of theological and ecclesiological thinking which exists in the Church of Scotland.**

An old friend of mine used to speak of people who were "so heavenly-minded that they were no earthly use" and of those who were "so earthly minded that they were of no heavenly good." For me, the right perspective lies somewhere in between and it is beautifully expressed in Eugene Peterson's paraphrase quoted below.

So, if you're serious about living this new resurrection life with Christ, act like it. Pursue the things over which Christ presides. Don't shuffle along, eyes to the ground, absorbed with the things right in front of you. Look up, and be alert to what is going on around Christ - that's where the action is. See things from his perspective.

Colossians 3.1-2, The Message

Those who are committed to the life of a disciple can find satisfaction and growth in body, mind and soul. It is the holistic approach that leads to a mature faith and that helps us to see the world through the eyes of Christ. Nothing could be more important than properly equipping the leadership of the Church to engage in a witness that is both spiritual in nature and yet bears all the hallmarks of a Christ-like humanity.

That is why I am delighted to welcome the Learn initiative in general and the *Eldership* publication in particular as it seeks to deepen our knowledge in the things of the faith and to strengthen those who have the awesome responsibility of leading the Church at a particularly challenging time of change.

One of the strengths of this publication is that it draws on the great breadth and diversity of theological and ecclesiological thinking which exists in the Church of Scotland. No single approach to Church life and no one account of theology is enough for a Church which is national, territorial and above all living; so, I hope you derive much through the different articles and diverse ideas that are presented in this publication.

Why not gather together as a group of elders over lunch and go through the different articles, and then plot out a programme for the way in which you will continue to learn from and support one another in your work. I cannot emphasise enough how well equipped you have to be to meet the challenge of sharing the faith against the prevailing mood and culture of our time.

As a Church we are living in challenging and changing times – so "don't shuffle along, eyes to the ground, absorbed with the things right in front of you", equip yourself to defend the faith; become confident that God has not been rendered obsolete and "be alert to what is going on around Christ – that's where the action is".

Finally, let me express the thanks of the whole Church of Scotland to those who have contributed richly to this publication. The writers have come from a variety of traditions in the Church of Scotland, but all of them are deeply rooted in the life of their local congregations, so their reflections come from real-life Church. I hope that they will be an inspiration to you as you build real, live Church in your congregation and community. ∎

DECLARATION

The following is taken from
The Ordination and Admission of Elders.

In this act,
the Church of Scotland,
as part of the holy catholic or universal Church,
worshipping one God,
Father, Son, and Holy Spirit
affirms anew its belief
in the Gospel
of the sovereign grace and love of God,
wherein through Jesus Christ,
his only Son, our Lord,
incarnate, crucified, and risen,
he freely offers to all,
upon repentance and faith,
the forgiveness of sins,
renewal by the Holy Spirit,
and eternal life,
and calls them to labour
in the fellowship of faith
for the advancement of the kingdom of God
throughout the world.

The Church of Scotland
acknowledges the Word of God,
contained in the Scriptures
of the Old and New Testaments,
to be the supreme rule of faith and life.
The Church of Scotland
holds as its subordinate standard
the Westminster Confession of Faith,
recognising liberty of opinion
on such points of doctrine
as do not enter into the substance of the Faith,
and claiming the right,
in dependence on the promised guidance
of the Holy Spirit,
to formulate, interpret,
or modify its subordinate standards:
always in agreement with the Word of God
and the fundamental doctrines
of the Christian faith
contained in the Confession,
of which agreement
the Church itself shall be sole judge.

AFFIRMATION

Do you believe in the fundamental doctrines of the Christian faith;
Do you promise to seek the unity and peace of this Church;
To uphold its doctrine, worship, government and discipline;
And to take your due part in the administration of its affairs?

I do.

Taken from Order for the Ordination and Admission of Elders found in the
Church of Scotland's *The Book of Common Order* (p.333). www.standrewpress.com

Waking,
awareness,
setting out on our spiritual journey,
the inner pilgrimage,
to discover God and discover ourselves anew,
by the guidance of the Holy Spirit,
framed within the gospel of renewing love,
and held by the One who transcends the world.
Holy God,
Father, Son and Holy Spirit,
tenderly, delicately,
lead us in discernment of our call,
in the certain knowledge that You are ahead of us,
waiting to greet us.

Loosen our hearts,
help us to risk our worth,
celebrate and share our gifting,
love with enthusiasm and, again,
succumb to Your acceptance of us,
and Your limitless forgiveness.

Grant us strength, honesty and commitment
in taking our vow;
underpin our vocation with humility,
sensitivity, energy and, in all our decision-making,
may our motives be pure,
our language measured,
and our care for others paramount.

There is no greater calling than to be a follower of Jesus:
in helping others to be the people of God,
may we find our fulfilment, our completion, in Christ.

Amen.

Rev Scott S. McKenna, Mayfield Salisbury Parish Church, www.mayfieldsalisbury.org

IS AN ELDER?

Andrew I M Kimmitt
Church of Scotland Candidate for Ministry, University of Aberdeen

What is an elder?

There is a distinct and peculiar prominence of the elder in Presbyterian Churches, which take their very name from the biblical Greek word translated as elder: *presbyteros*. In 1964, immediately after the admission of women to the eldership, the Church of Scotland stated that "The office of elder is one of the spiritual offices of the Church of Scotland and is concerned with the oversight and pastoral work of a congregation."[1] That simple, neat and accurate formula is a good way to begin the story of a complex, occasionally controversial, history and theology underpinning the ministry of eldership in the Church of Scotland.

Origins of the eldership

As the movement of the Reformation unfolded across Europe, bringing with it vast changes in social and Church life in many places, the Reformation leaders were exercised with finding the best (which meant most Scripturally appropriate) way of organising the ministry of the Church. Confronted with Bible passages that spoke of "elders" in various ways, Reformers took different approaches. Martin Luther understood the elders of the Bible simply to mean "one who is generally an older person"[2] and left the matter there. In contrast, John Calvin drew on passages like Exodus 3.16 and 1 Timothy 5.17 to conclude that the Church required the office of presbyters who undertook the government and rule of the Church. The difficulty in Calvin's teaching is not whether there should be a ministry of eldership involving the "rule" of the Church, but who should undertake it. Calvin understood that the office of presbyter should only be held by ordained ministers of Word and Sacrament, despite the fact that he included some elected "lay seniors" (normally lawyers and magistrates) onto a body exercising spiritual discipline in Geneva.[3]

Calvin taught that Christ's "true" Church was present wherever the Word of God was preached faithfully and the sacraments were rightly administered. John Knox, a pupil of Calvin in Geneva, added a third "mark": the true Church existed where spiritual discipline was upheld.[4] This emphasis on upholding discipline saw the beginnings of a merger between the office of presbyter and the "lay seniors" who helped exercise discipline. Knox's model of Reformation Scotland set forth in *The First Book of Discipline* demanded the annual election of elders who should be "of best knowledge of God's word, or cleanest life... to assist the minister in all public affairs of the church".[5] Under Knox's leadership, elders were neither ordained nor expected to serve for life. Later commentators have called this the "lay theory" of eldership.

Ordination of elders and the "presbyter theory" of eldership

A significant change, the introduction of "presbyter theory", occurred in 1578 with Andrew Melville's work on eldership set out in *The Second Book of Discipline*. Even though Knox had intended that elders should be elected for one year only, in practice many were re-elected repeatedly.[6] By contrast, Melville advocated the election and ordination for life of elders, whom he understood to have equal status with ministers. Both groups exercised the spiritual ministry of a presbyter but they differed in function: ministers were elders who taught, while other elders provided ruling oversight.[7] The office of the elder was transformed from being an elected annual helper to being a permanent vocation recognised by public ordination. Melville outlined the key duties of an elder: "chiefly the teaching of the Word"; "watching over the flock committed to them"; "reaping the fruit of the Word sown by the ministers"; "examining those coming to the Lord's table", "executing the Acts of the General Assembly"; and "holding assemblies with the ministers to ensure good order of the Church".[8] This job description has remained constant since 1578, even if intervening years have seen near constant argument over what an elder ought to be. Such debates broadly stem from the difference between the "lay" and "presbyter" theories outlined above.

Recent understandings of the elder

The most radical and thorough proposals in recent times have been provided by revered Scottish theologian Very Rev Prof T. F. Torrance who advocated abandoning discipline as an essential "mark" of the Church, understanding the ministry of the true Church to be shaped only around Word and Sacrament.[9] For Torrance, ordained ministers should be thought of as providing Word and Sacrament to the people of God while lay elders are there to enable an appropriate response from the people of God. For Torrance, the confusion between lay (elders) and ordained (ministers) developed through misreading Scripture "with a presbyterian lens".[10]

In 1989, the General Assembly heard a report on eldership that followed Torrance's thought very closely, containing suggestions that a congregation should elect elders democratically for a fixed term of between 5 and 10 years with enforced sabbaticals and that elders should no longer be ordained to the office. The report was dismissed and considered to be devaluing to the eldership.[11] In 2001, the General Assembly revisited the subject of eldership, this time affirming its status as an ordained ministry and outlining four criteria for any form of ordained ministry: 1) they are not to be concerned with just one part of the Church's life but with keeping the Church to its true nature and calling; 2) they are to be ministries of the universal Church; 3) they are to be ministries whose vocation is affirmed and tested by the Church; 4) they are to be ministries which endure through time.[12] This was followed by a 2003 report by the Assembly Council, which was instructed to "enable the whole church to rediscover the full significance of the eldership as a spiritual office".[13] Responding to a consultation on how this might be achieved, elders expressed a great desire for ongoing training: in pastoral care, leading worship, music ministry, youth work, and mission.[14] In particular, elders called for a renewed emphasis upon the spiritual nature of the office.

So, where are we today? A question remains as to the role of the elder and the role of discipline within the Church of Scotland. The role of the eldership is also affected by a sense of urgency in the Church as it recognises the need to reach beyond its membership in mission: the potential breadth of talents elders might employ was given a prominent place when the Church of Scotland determined to be a "church without walls". The current understanding of an elder is broadly in line with Melville's job description of "tending to the flock" of the congregation and "reaping the fruit of the Word sown by the ministers". The office of elder remains central to our Presbyterian identity and has an enduring and vital role to play in the spiritual and pastoral oversight in the Church of Scotland. ■

Questions for discussion

1. Do you think ordination is an important aspect of eldership?
2. What do you regard as the similarities and differences between the elder and the minister?
3. What, for you, are the key aspects of being an elder?

Further reading

- Stewart Matthew and Kenneth B. Scott, **Leading God's People: a handbook for elders** (Edinburgh: Saint Andrew Press, 1995)
- Stewart Matthew and Ken Lawson, **Caring for God's People: a handbook for elders and ministers on pastoral care** (Edinburgh: Saint Andrew Press, 1995)
- See **www.churchofscotland.org.uk/learn** for more on eldership.

Why not try... identifying a personal highlight so far of being an elder and note the lessons for your ministry? What characteristics in other elders have inspired you?

1   Church of Scotland Panel on Doctrine, *The Office of Elder in the Church of Scotland*, (Edinburgh: Saint Andrew Press, 1964), p.1.
2   Martin Luther quoted in James Kirk's commentary upon *The Second Book of Discipline* (Edinburgh: Saint Andrew Press, 1980), footnote p.191.
3   See Thomas F. Torrance, *Gospel, Church, and Ministry* (Eugene: Pickwick Publications, 1984/2012), pp.183-184.
4   See G.D. Henderson and James Bulloch, *Scots Confession of 1560*, (Edinburgh: Saint Andrew Press, 2007), chapter 168.
5   See *The First Book of Discipline* (Edinburgh: St. Andrew Press, 1972), heading 8, p.174.
6   James Kirk, 'Introduction' to *The Second Book of Discipline*, p.88.
7   James Kirk, 'Introduction' to *The Second Book of Discipline*, p.93.
8   James Kirk, *The Second Book of Discipline*, heading 4, pp.191-193.
9   See Thomas F. Torrance, *Gospel, Church, and Ministry*, p.199.
10 See Thomas F. Torrance, *Gospel, Church, and Ministry*, p.199.
11 Douglas Murray, "Recent Debate on the Eldership in the Church of Scotland" in Lukas Vischer (ed.), *The Ministry of the Elders in the Reformed Church* (Berne: Evangelische Arbeitsstelle Oekumene Schweiz, 1992), pp.193-196.
12 Report of the Panel on Doctrine to the General Assembly of the Church of Scotland, 2001.
13 Report of the Assembly Council to the General Assembly of the Church of Scotland, 2003, 11/9, paragraph 4.1.1.
14 Report of the Assembly Council to the General Assembly of the Church of Scotland, 2003, 11/10, paragraph 4.2.

OUR CHURCH BY NUMBERS

1 FAITH LORD CHURCH

AROUND **400,000** MEMBERS

32 HIV & AIDS PROJECTS SUPPORTED IN **16** COUNTRIES

OVER **1,300** CONGREGATIONS

OVER **32,500** ELDERS
51.5% FEMALE
48.5% MALE

16 MISSION PARTNERS

OVER 300 READERS

OVER 23,000 MEMBERS OF THE GUILD IN OVER 900 GROUPS

IN 2013...
OVER **3000** WEDDINGS
OVER **4000** BAPTISMS
OVER **24,000** FUNERALS

190 TWINNINGS WITH PARTNER CHURCHES

OVER 40 ORDAINED LOCAL MINISTERS

OVER **800** MINISTERS

56 PARTNER CHURCHES ACROSS THE WORLD

OVER 100 MINISTRIES DEVELOPMENT STAFF

OVER 70 SERVICES SUPPORTING VULNERABLE PEOPLE IN SCOTLAND THROUGH CROSSREACH

46 PRESBYTERIES INCLUDING ENGLAND, EUROPE AND JERUSALEM.

THE ROAD ELDERS

Laurence Wareing

Freelance writer, www.laurencew.org

The road to eldership is paved with many questions such as "Why me?" and "What does it involve?", and those implicit ones that sometimes lie behind the statement: "But I'm not good enough".

In *Reflections on Eldership* (Saint Andrew Press) many of those who responded to my questions would be hard-pressed to tell you of a clear moment of calling to this ministry of the Church; rather, they describe a process of question, reassurance and exploration.

One example in the book of an elder's sense of call reveals a profound ambiguity that I overlooked at the time. This elder speaks of walking along the Via Dolorosa in Jerusalem, retracing the steps of Jesus as he carried his cross towards Calvary. "The tour guide pointed out the station of the cross where Simon of Cyrene was press-ganged into carrying Christ's cross," he remembers. "I felt very moved and vowed to do more to serve my Lord." He is describing a clear moment of decision, even revelation. Yet at the heart of it is that phrase "press-ganged," and I'm reminded of the woman who told me about being "accosted" in the street by an interim minister and persuaded, despite all the other ongoing commitments and difficulties in her life, to become an elder.

I was struck by the words of an elder from the Scottish islands who cautions against over-eagerness to put one's name forward. Awareness of our own gifts and contributions should always be tempered, he implies, by humility.

Indeed humility, as well as self-doubt, can be a factor behind that refrain, "I'm not good enough" – a close cousin of the more biblical-sounding "Lord, why me?" Memorably, one man recalled the elders he would observe "dressed in black on a Sunday" (black is still perceived as the default dress-code of elders by many) "and sat in a holy huddle in front of the pulpit ... Those people were so good, they almost had wings on. I couldn't be like that." In reality, few of us can – even those who appear as angels in our own eyes. Remembering Jesus' own followers (and the prophets who preceded them), there is something reassuringly biblical about that realisation.

Elders are not experts; or rather, they are not expert at being elders. "You have a fabric committee that has the right people on it – architects, electricians," one elder told me; "you have a social committee that can basically feed the five thousand; you have a finance committee that has the right people on it, who know about money. And then you have a Session... I think the Session should be spiritual ...". The calling to eldership is the calling to discernment, to the support of pastoral ministry and to the care of God's children. It is not, as one woman observed, about being another committee person – "It is much more important."

Eldership embodies not perfection but aspiration: the willingness to do one's best. Another Church member, invited to consider taking on the role, anticipated the prospect of "quiet, dignified service, requiring some sacrifice, much tact,

O TO HIP

and the setting of a constant good example ..." "Willingness to do one's best seemed to be all that mattered," observed another.

One person's best may not be the same as another's, of course. A number of people I spoke to echoed words from the 2001 General Assembly report known as "A Church Without Walls". It called for us to develop the diverse gifts of potential elders and not to persist in squeezing square pegs into round holes. The life of the eldership may well push you out of your comfort zone, but it will not necessarily demand that you be moulded into a fixed list of duties. Indeed, as the Church of Scotland increasingly explores different and imaginative ways of ministering to the people of Scotland, eldership will be re-crafted to meet local needs and national imperatives.

More than ever, it seems to me, the road that leads towards the eldership is not one that ends at a fixed destination. The sometimes daunting notion that this is about ordination for life turns out to be a gift, because accepting a call to the eldership is not about coming to the table fully-formed; rather, it is about the willingness to model life-long learning. Our questions ("Why me?"; "What will this demand of me?") will not be answered with direct responses but through lived experience and shared reflection. The questions won't go away but the answers will continue to grow and evolve. ∎

Questions for discussion

1. Consider some characters from the Bible who were called. Are there any with whom you identify and why?
2. Are there any characters that you find challenging? What aspects of their call to service would you find difficult?
3. Prayerfully reflect on the role of being an elder. Make a note of the strengths and characteristics that you think make a good elder. Note down the hopes you have about serving within your congregation.

✚ Further reading

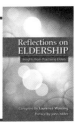

- Laurence Wareing (ed.), **Reflections on Eldership: insights from practising elders** (Edinburgh: Saint Andrew Press, 2014).

 Why not try... asking one or two different elders about their experience of the eldership? You may find it helpful to do this over a coffee or a meal, concluding your conversation with prayer.

DISCERNING A CALL TO ELDERSHIP

Ruth Harvey

Place for Hope, www.placeforhope.org.uk

Introduction: What is discernment?

How do we know when we have a "calling" from God? What is the difference between God speaking to us, and our own desire, prejudice or anxiety speaking to us? These are constant questions, pondered by such luminaries as Ignatius of Loyola in the 15th century, and Joan Chittister in the 21st century. We are in good company as we ask: am I called to this ministry?

Ignatius, a soldier in the Spanish army, was injured in battle. During his convalescence he read *The Life of Christ*, and did much day dreaming. In the process, he discovered that God was speaking to him through these day dreams. This led to a period of reflection during which he came to the realisation that he had the gift of discernment. He day dreamed about serving a king different from the earthly King of Spain. And these dreams left him feeling inspired, energised and eager. What gave him consolation resulted in a full, rounded sense of satisfaction. This experience of discernment became a lifelong vocation of discovering God, self and the world. Through this experience of reflection, he was drawn into the service of God. There is much to be gained from reflection on Ignatius' life and faith.[1]

When it comes to the question of discerning God's call there are many stories to draw on. What for one person can feel like being taken to the brink of a cliff, for another can feel like standing on a safe balcony overlooking a magnificent view. Further, calling can involve a strong sense of clarity about vision and purpose and at once feel daunting, terrifying and delightfully awe-inspiring. Either way, it is worth remembering that God is always ahead of us, whatever decision we make.

A Discernment Toolkit

Here are some suggestions for a "discernment toolkit". Like any good toolkit, we should be able to dip into it, to find treasures, tools, techniques that are in good working order, some of which may be appropriate for the task in hand. And a good toolkit always has room for more new tools to be added. Here are three tools for exploring a call to the eldership:

1. **Journaling:** This is a way of capturing our own thoughts, feelings and insights. Used as part of our regular prayer time, a journal can be a very powerful tool for understanding our own sense of call, and of God's purpose for our lives. If writing words doesn't flow for you, try doodling – images can often tell a story.

2. **Skills and gifts:** consider the difference between your skills and your gifts. Consider the possibility that your skills are what you learn through life, and that your gifts are intrinsic abilities. Working to your skills, while important, might leave you depleted and tired. Working to your gifts, on the other hand, might leave you weary but energised. When considering your sense of call, ask yourself if there is a healthy balance between working to your gifts and to your skills.

3. **God/self/community:** Consider the balance between a calling from God, from self and from your community. Noticing a convergence, a balance between these three interlocking circles can be a prompt that you are being led, or "called" in a particular direction.

  - **Calling from God:** time spent in prayer can bring unexpected insights. By prayerfully reading a passage of scripture we are open to being surprised by the Holy Spirit. Find a safe, uninterrupted space to settle. Perhaps light a candle. Read a favourite passage of Scripture. Hold some silence. Read the passage once more. Ask God to speak to you. Be open to what comes to you. Perhaps spend some time journaling your thoughts. Practice regularly.

  - **Calling from self:** stay alert to how you feel about the possibilities within a decision. Think through the pros and cons of an option. Maybe make a list or draw a diagram of the "plusses" and "minuses" involved. Imagine you have made a decision one way, or the other. Consider how you would feel – full of dread, or full of possibility. Does the thought of one course of action make your hands feel sweaty, give you goose bumps, or fill your heart with joy? Invite God to speak to you through your intellect, and through your body.

  - **Calling from community:** be alert to the promptings of your friends and family. Share your thoughts with others, and listen carefully to the considered responses of those whom you trust. Ask them for prayerful support. Notice if your name is suggested or if you are consistently volunteered for a position that recognises your gifts. Don't allow embarrassment or fear to smother the gifts that God has given you, and that others recognise in you. ■

 Questions for discussion

1. Remember a time when you were absolutely clear that you had made the right decision. Consider your feelings and your thoughts at that time. How would you describe that feeling of clarity?
2. Consider the following passages and questions that reflect on "calling" and "discernment":
   a. Isaiah 6.1-8. To what is God calling you?
   b. Acts 6. How are you being called to be a channel of God's love?
   c. Luke 10.1-17. How does this passage speak to you about a collective calling?
   d. Matthew 28.16-20. In what ways is this commission of Jesus part of your own calling?
3. In what ways are you called by God, by yourself, by your community? Notice the areas of convergence.

 Further reading

· Patricia Loring, **Spiritual Discernment** (Philadelphia: Pendle Hill Publications, 1993)
· Joan Chittister, **Following the Path: the search for a life of passion, purpose and joy** (New York: Image, 2012)
· Rough Guide to Exploring Ministries (2012) Further Ministries Team, **www.furtherministriesteam.com/exploringministries.pdf.**

 Why not try... keeping a spiritual journal? Find a journal that you will enjoy using. Jot down thoughts, doodles, ideas that reflect your spiritual life. Choose a time and a place to journal that will help you focus.

1   See Margaret Silf, *Inner Compass: an invitation to Ignatian spirituality*, (Chicago: Loyola Press, 1999).

Meaning and mystery,
stars and stories,
Absence and Presence,
Holy God,
You reveal Yourself
through the wonder and complexity of creation,
through sacred Scripture and imagination, and
through creeds, confessions and the continuing evolution of thought.

You are the Sound at the centre of the world,
the Silence echoing across the universe,
the elusive Spirit,
found in the Word, written and preached,
in the grace of water, wine and wheat,
and in the compassionate care of companionship.

Present too in the soul of Your people,
Your gospel in myriad forms
across two thousand years
shared among apostles, mystics, evangelists and common saints,
aid us on our inner journey,
strengthen us in our faith,
deepen our trust in the Risen, ascended Christ,
the Spirit of Jesus beside us
and within.

Amen.

Rev Scott S. McKenna, Mayfield Salisbury Parish Church, www.mayfieldsalisbury.org

CONSIDERING WHAT WE BELIEVE

An excerpt from Articles Declaratory of the Constitution
of the Church of Scotland.

The Church of Scotland is part of the Holy Catholic or Universal Church; worshipping one God, Almighty, all-wise, and all-loving, in the Trinity of the Father, the Son, and the Holy Ghost, the same in substance, equal in power and glory; adoring the Father, infinite in Majesty, of whom are all things; confessing our Lord Jesus Christ, the Eternal Son, made very man for our salvation; glorying in His Cross and Resurrection, and owning obedience to Him as the Head over all things to His Church; trusting in the promised renewal and guidance of the Holy Spirit; proclaiming the forgiveness of sins and acceptance with God through faith in Christ, and the gift of Eternal Life; and labouring for the advancement of the kingdom of God throughout the world. The Church of Scotland adheres to the Scottish Reformation; receives the Word of God which is contained in the Scriptures of the Old and New Testaments as its supreme rule of faith and life; and avows the fundamental doctrines of the Catholic faith founded thereupon. ■

Please note: this is not a creedal statement. The Articles Declaratory of the Church's constitution lay out our structure, how we govern and membership details. Read the full document here: www.churchofscotland.org.uk/about_us/church_law/church_constitution

 Why not try... reading the Statements of the Church's faith?
Find it at: **www.churchofscotland.org.uk/about_us/our_faith/ statements_of_the_churchs_faith** Here you will find The Apostles' Creed and the 1992 A Statement of Christian Faith.

Statement of Christian Faith cards available at: **www.standrewpress.com**

THE AUTHORITY OF THE CREEDS

Frances Henderson

Minister of Hoddom, Kirtle-Eaglesfield & Middlebie Church,
Presbytery of Annandale & Eskdale

A young 16th-century monk by the name of Martin Luther was outraged by some of the practices within the Church that he considered to be highly dubious, for example "indulgences". In his famous "Ninety-Five Theses" he accused the Church of adding "human doctrines" to the faith which had been given by God. As the Protestant Reformation progressed, Luther's objections developed into a principle called *sola scriptura* – by scripture alone.

The problem is that sometimes the doctrine of *sola scriptura* is over-simplified, so that you might hear some Christians say that "all you need is the Bible". This is not what the Protestant Reformers meant at all. The Reformers were well aware that the Bible needs to be explained properly, otherwise we could come away with misguided ideas about God and what God requires of us. Even nowadays, there are "Churches" that require snake-handling as a test of faith.

IT IS A WAY OF AFFIRMING THE FAITH THAT UNITES ALL CHRISTIANS ACROSS THE WORLD...

More than 1,000 years prior to Luther, the early Church was faced with problems of how to understand the Scripture. Their debates and decisions have come down to us in the form of the creeds. Several creeds were written, but the two which have become the most significant are the Apostles' Creed and the Nicene Creed. The Nicene Creed was agreed at a Church council in 325AD, and then was modified and expanded by a later council in 381AD. Less is known about the origins of the Apostles' Creed but its origins are believed to be earlier than the Nicene Creed.

Creeds, like all theology, are a product of their time. The early Church spent a long time working out what Scripture says about Jesus when they call him "the Son of God". Many explanations were offered seriously and in good faith, but after discussion these were deemed to be inadequate in some way, and so were called "heresies". For example, one such heresy was called "docetism". Docetism was the belief that Jesus was so divine that he was barely human at all: his feet did not touch the ground when he walked, and he did not die on the cross (because gods can't die!). By contrast, the Apostles' Creed stresses the humanness of Jesus alongside his divinity, so that the Church that recites it regularly should not make that mistake again.

The Apostles' Creed and the Nicene Creed were decided at a time when there was still "one Church" before any of the later schisms. This is why they are often called the "Ecumenical Creeds", because they are accepted as authoritative by every mainstream Christian Church. (Although as far as we know, the Apostles' Creed was never accepted by an Ecumenical Council like that of Nicea, and so it is not held in the same regard by the Eastern Orthodox Churches.) This makes the Creeds very important for Christian unity.

That is not to say that every Christian can agree with every statement in the creeds. For one thing, the Nicene Creed is written with the help of philosophical language of the day, and some theologians have argued that it should be rewritten in language better suited to more contemporary ways of thinking. Also, in the light of modern science, many Christians find that they struggle with the idea of the Virgin Birth, or the Resurrection of the Dead. Some may resolve this problem by interpreting the creeds in a more metaphorical or symbolic way. This means that two Christians, standing side by side and saying the creed together, might nevertheless be meaning two quite different things.

The creeds, as they stand, remain authoritative and binding for us as Christians. They indicate to us which Churches are truly Christian or not, and they tell us what we must sign up to if we want to call ourselves Christian – although there may still be room for interpretation. We can, of course, have doubts and questions about various parts of the creeds and still be a Christian, but we cannot redefine the faith for ourselves. We do not have that authority. The Church of Scotland regards the creeds as less authoritative than the Bible but still important within our Church life. Unlike the Bible, but like the Westminster Confession, these early creeds are not "set in stone", and potentially they could be altered. However, this could likely only be done by the decision of another Ecumenical Council. As this would require the meeting and agreement of the whole Church across the world, this is not likely to happen. By contrast, the Church of Scotland and its various "daughter" churches, such as the Presbyterian Church (USA), have adjusted the Westminster Confession in the past.

All this is why many Church of Scotland churches will recite one or other of the creeds at services of baptism and communion. There is a great value in all standing together and proclaiming these ancient words. It is a way of affirming the faith that unites all Christians across the world and across time, for the creeds are a direct link with the faith of our ancestors. And it means that you can go to any church of any tradition and find that you are saying these same words together. ∎

Note: You can find the Apostles' Creed at Hymn 628, and the Nicene Creed at Hymn 649 in the *Church Hymnary Fourth Edition* (London: Canterbury Press, 2005).

 Questions for discussion

1. Does your local church ever recite one or other of the creeds? Do you think this is something worth doing?
2. Should the creeds be rewritten to reflect more modern ways of thinking?
3. What should Christians do if they find parts of the creeds difficult to accept?

 Further reading

· William Barclay, **The Apostles' Creed** (Louisville: Westminster John Knox Press, 1998)
· J.N.D. Kelly, **Early Christian Creeds** (London & New York: Bloomsbury Publishing, 2006).

 Why not try... writing your own "I believe" summary of your Christian faith?

OUR FOUNDATIONAL TEXT:
THE BIBLE

Alison Jack

Assitant Principal of New College, University of Edinburgh

In the Church of Scotland, as in other Churches, we affirm that the Bible is our foundational text, but just how are we to approach this key text? An answer to this question might consider the sweep of the story the Bible tells, from Creation in Genesis, to Re-creation in Revelation. Or it might offer something of the story of the Bible itself, the process by which it came to be written and collected, seeking to answer questions such as "Why are there four Gospels, and not just one account of the life of Jesus?" Another option would be to consider the ways in which the Bible has influenced our culture and literature.

So many possible approaches to the one text: and that is what makes the Bible so fascinating.

Perhaps the complexity of the Bible and its story, however, means it can also be a daunting prospect actually to open the Bible and begin to read it. We hear short extracts each Sunday, and hope to have them explained in the sermon, but perhaps we miss a sense of any overall picture. And we are encouraged to assume that the Bible is for experts, who have studied its difficulties and formed opinions about its meaning. I want to encourage you to open your Bibles and start to read. To guide you in the task, I want to suggest some themes to look out for, which will help you to make sense of what you are reading.

One key theme is exile: being taken from home and the longing to return. We see it in the physical exile of much of the Jewish community after their defeat by the Babylonians, referred to in Jeremiah 39-43, the end of 2 Kings, 2 Chronicles and Daniel 1-6, and their homecoming described in Ezra. This exile is foreshadowed in the time of slavery in Egypt, from which God delivers the people through the leadership of Moses, detailed in Exodus. In Matthew (2.13-15), Jesus and his family are exiled to Egypt. The younger son in the Parable of the Prodigal Son enters a self-imposed exile in a "far country" (Luke 15.13). In the apocalyptic sections of Matthew 24 and Luke 18.7, there is a sense of the followers of Jesus being far from home, and waiting for deliverance. 1 Peter 1.1 makes a direct connection between believers and the exiled; and, of course, the writer of the Book of Revelation, John, describes himself as having been exiled on the remote island of Patmos (1.9), and presents a picture of the dramatic process whereby God will bring his people "home". The theme of exile speaks of longing and of things not being right; it assumes a notion of "home", secured by God, and hopes for safe return under the protection of one chosen by God. It is a powerful image which is found in many places in the Bible.

Another theme is the overturning of expectations, often involving the privileging of the poorest and weakest. We see this in the unexpected rise to power of the youngest and least likely candidates: Jacob rather than his older twin Esau; Joseph rather than an older brother; Moses with his speech impediment; Esther, a slave girl in a foreign land; David with his slingshot against the giant Goliath; Mary's song in Luke 1.46-55, echoing Hannah's song after the birth of Samuel (1 Samuel 2.1-10), in which the rich are sent away hungry but the poor are fed. Many of the parables depend on this reversal of fortunes, the surprise ending: think of the parable of the workers in the vineyard (Matthew 20) or the most famous of all, the Good Samaritan (Luke 10.29-37). Although it is less shocking to us than it would have been to their first readers, Matthew, Mark and Luke present Jesus privileging children over adults ("Let the children come to me, and do not try to stop them. For the kingdom of God belongs to such as these" (Luke 18.16)). Paul boasts of his scholarship and impeccable standing in the Jewish community, but counts it all as rubbish compared to knowing Jesus (Philippians 3). What humans call wisdom, Paul writes, is foolishness to God (1 Corinthians 3.19); and it is through the death of Jesus, the most ignominious death imaginable, on a cross like a common criminal, that resurrection becomes possible and salvation is somehow secured. The Bible is full of such surprises and paradoxes.

A third theme to look out for is robust engagement with God. Moses pleads with God on behalf of the people, who have fashioned and worshipped the

 Questions for discussion

1. Are there other Bible stories that are powerful for you and that have exile or engagement with God as a theme?
2. What other narrative threads running through the Bible particularly strike you?
3. Share a story in the Bible which you find troubling, or puzzling, and discuss what it might have meant to its first readers; and what it might mean for us today.

 Further reading

· Stephen Harris, **Understanding the Bible**, 7th edition (Boston: McGraw Hill, 2007)
· Excellent and accessible lectures on many biblical topics are available online from Open Yale Courses: **http://oyc.yale.edu**

New Testament:
· Mark Allan Powell, **Introducing the New Testament: a historical, literary and theological survey** (Grand Rapids: Baker Academic Press, 2009).

Old Testament:
· John Drane, **Introducing the Old Testament**, 3rd edition (Oxford: Lion Press, 2011)
· For those who prefer a narrative approach, try Bruce Longenecker's novel, **The Lost Letters of Pergamum** (Grand Rapids: Baker Academic Press, 2003).

 Why not try... reading a chapter or two of Luke's Gospel, or a Psalm, each day for the next week?

golden calf; and an angry God relents (Exodus 32). Job, in his misery and with the unhelpful theorising of his friends ringing in his ears, engages with God to try to make sense of what has happened to him. The Psalmist speaks words of lament which have resonated throughout the centuries, unafraid to express a sense of hopelessness and despair: "Awake, Lord! Why do you sleep? Rouse yourself! Do not reject us forever. Why do you hide your face and forget our misery and oppression?" (Psalm 44.12-13). Luke's Jesus, on the Mount of Olives, pleads with God to take away the fate he knows awaits him (Luke 22.43-44); Matthew's Jesus in agony on the cross makes Psalm 22 his own, demanding to know why God has forsaken him (Matthew 27.45-46). The Bible does not protect its readers from the widest range of human experience, both positive and negative and, most significantly, it validates authentic responses of anger, questioning and doubt.

With these themes in mind, where is the best place to start reading? First, find a translation which suits your reading preference: for clarity and directness, try the Good News Version; for something a little more nuanced, try the New Revised Standard Version. If you want the buzz of the fresh and vigorous, and don't mind the Americanisms, try The Message. And then open it at Luke's Gospel, perhaps the most elegant and uncluttered of the gospels, offering a story of Jesus told by a skilled narrator. In the Old Testament, Genesis and Exodus offer the foundational narratives of the Jewish and Christian faiths: here you will find Adam and Eve, Abraham and Sarah, Joseph and his brothers, Moses in his basket and Pharaoh with his hardened heart, not willing to let the people go. Seek out the stories, let your eyes skim over geographical and genealogical detail for now. The Book of Acts, although it meanders somewhat, gives a sense of the formation of the early Church. The Letter to the Philippians offers Paul at his best, full of uplifting and encouraging advice to the fledgling Church he founded.

Read these texts afresh, looking out for common themes, and you will find riches indeed: a deeper understanding of the faith, of who Jesus was and is, and of ways to be a Christian in today's world. ∎

OUR FOUNDATIONAL ACT: PRAYER

Roddy Hamilton

Minister of New Kilpatrick Church, Presbytery of Dumbarton

It is too easy to speak of "types" of prayer, or read manuals about how to pray, or gather anthologies of the many varied prayers from our own and other traditions to repeat as if we can perfect our prayer. Prayer is rather more fundamental than style. Essentially it is a way of being – a way of living in the world that faithfully notices, reflects, supports, and encourages the life of the world with the hopes of God's Reign. It might be words. It might be silence. It might be a groan in our souls, but whatever prayer sounds like, it is the connecting of ourselves with God and to the world, and being the light of love in whatever place we find ourselves. Leonard Cohen famously describes how light permeates everything through the cracks.

When Jesus prayed, we know he often used words, but there were many times, in the wee small hours of the morning, that we find him in silence, on his own. We might also say that when Jesus healed that was prayer, when Jesus preached that was prayer. There will always be times when we use formal language and style in our spoken prayers in the leading of worship but these prayers are just the part of the iceberg that rises above the surface of the water. The greater part of prayer is the whole living we do, the longings we hold, that response we make to news headlines, the silence we find in pain and the laughter and celebration we share in community. This is the way Jesus' whole life was lived, and in these ways we become the connecting places of love.

To pray, we need to live in the world fully with the headlines in one hand and the Gospel in the other. To pray, we immerse ourselves in the pain of others and the joys too, without the need to find some formula with words. To pray, we become aware of our connection with the world, and we have an increasing awareness and trust in the story of transformation, renewal and resurrection.

Our foundational act of prayer is not just a traditional moment early in the morning or evening where everything else is quiet, but a robust and full engagement with life and all it offers us. It is not about the words we use but the relationships through which we grow with the world. It is not about the worry and the difficulty in finding words when we sit with people; in fact it has little to do with words at all. It is the spontaneous urge we have to refocus what we see happening and experience, and to cry out for the promises of God. That is the space, the crack, that lets the light get in. ■

 Questions for discussion

1. What makes prayer difficult for you?
2. What resources or experiences might help in our prayerful lives?
3. How have you experienced God's 'light' getting into a particular situation?

 Further reading

- **The Year Without Prayer** (2012) www.faith-theology.com/2012/07/the-year-without-prayer.html
- **re:Worship blogspot** (2014) http://re-worship.blogspot.co.uk [accessed 16th August 2014]
- Dave Tomlinson, **How to Be a Bad Christian** (London: Hodder & Stoughton, 2012), pp.135-144.

 Why not try... creating a prayer diary for a week that records the people you meet and the stories that speak most to you?

THE CHURCH AND THE ADVANCEMENT OF THE KINGDOM OF GOD

Tommy MacNeil
Minister of Martin's Memorial Church, Prebytery of Lewis

The Church remains important. Some question the validity of the Church and the influence we can have. That's nothing new. We need to focus on Christ and who he says we are and who he has called us to be as the Body of Christ.

I believe the Church of Scotland needs to re-discover the crucial and central role played by elders in the life and witness of the Church. Elders are often the unsung heroes in congregations. For me, they are like the missing pieces in the jigsaw. We know they are there, but at times they are not particularly visible. But the image of the Body of Christ (1 Cor 12.14-31) is incomplete without them. I believe we need to highlight our elders and celebrate who they are and the crucial role they fulfil. To help us consider the role of the elder and the kingdom of God I want to reflect briefly on three Biblical passages.

Let's begin with Exodus 17.1-6. The people of God are not in a good place. They are in a desert, a dry and desperate place. Moses, as God's appointed leader, is blamed for this predicament. The people murmur, complain, and quarrel with Moses. He is God's chosen vessel to lead the people from slavery to paradise. They acknowledged Moses as God's chosen servant when things were going well. Now they're not so sure. Sound familiar? The people are going beyond being thirsty; they are literally "dying for a drink". The people's verbal bashing of Moses quickly develops to the point where he is being threatened with death (v4b). What was he to do?

Moses cries out to God and in this place of desperate need God tells Moses to do three things: to walk on ahead of the people; take the staff of God in hand; and call some of the elders to stand with him (v5). This last instruction has important lessons for us today. Moses was surrounded by a multitude of people who were very unhappy with him and his leadership. He was called to lead God's people to a new destiny. In his predicament God made sure that when the going got tough, he did not have to stand alone. We learn that elders are to stand with and for God's leaders. I have no doubt that Moses' call to the elders to stand with him was not an easy one to respond to. So it may be with elders today. Elders are called to lead, support and stand with those God appoints to lead God's people on.

The beauty for the elders who stood with Moses is that they were the first to witness a great miracle as water began to flow from the Rock at Horeb (v6b). They saw the kingdom of God break forth as God made miraculous provision for the people. With that, they in turn were the first to have their thirst quenched, and they were then able to serve God with Moses in making sure the people's desperate need for life-giving water was met. In serving God and supporting God's leaders I believe elders can be expectant and excited for all that God wants to do through them. The kingdom of God comes to you to flow through you.

Now turn to Nehemiah 8.4-8. In these verses we see the restoration of God's purposes in the life experience of God's people. Having been in exile for many years, they return to a newly fortified Jerusalem. Ezra and Nehemiah were God's key leaders for this work. However, it is clear that they would not have been able to complete it without the practical and spiritual support of those who fulfilled the role of elders in their day. In v4 we are told of Ezra reading and preaching the Word of God to the people. He stood on a high platform built especially for the occasion so that the whole community who had gathered (v2) were afforded the opportunity of hearing the Word of God. At v4 we have a list of individuals who stood with Ezra as he read. We see here that the elders have a key role in supporting the preaching of the Word of God and sharing it with others.

Interestingly, the elders (and Levites) not only supported God's leaders in bringing God's word to God's people, they also had a crucial role in sharing and explaining Scripture so that all could understand (v8). Today, the Church of Scotland needs elders who will help leaders build places where the Word of God can be shared with all people. We need elders who are gifted in opening up the Word of God and sharing it with people both inside and outside of the Church.

Our final passage is Acts 20.22-38. Here we have a moving account by the apostle Paul on his departure from Ephesus. Paul had been in Ephesus for three years. In that time he had been faithful in preaching the Gospel to the people of that city. As he prepared to depart, it is clear that he had appointed elders to oversee and develop the work. These verses bring alive for us the power of elders in the church. They are involved in shepherding God's people and showing love to God's people. This teaches us of the important and unique role of elders in the context of local church life. Ministers will come and go, but elders are more constant and so fulfil a crucial role in bringing stability and continuity to the local congregation.

In Paul's plea to the elders at Ephesus we see the importance of shepherding God's people and the significance of the relationship between elder and minister. Paul prays with his friends and, as he does, they weep together, embrace one another, and even kiss one another (v37). In the New Testament Church this was the most obvious and natural expression of love. This is a picture of what Christ desires for the Church: a people who genuinely love one another. We are to show and share love with one another.

Elders, please be aware of the critical role you fulfil as you serve Christ in and through your local congregation and Presbytery. As you stand with and for God's servants, as you support the preaching of God's Word and share God's Word with others, and as you shepherd and show love to God's people you can expect to see more of God's kingdom coming to you and through you. Without you and your fellow elders, serving in the Church of Scotland, the Body of Christ would not be complete, and so the fullness of God's purposes would not be seen. ■

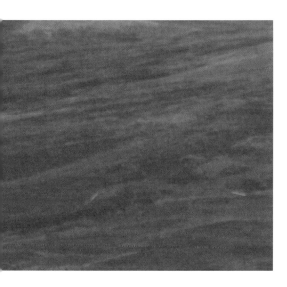

The Church of Scotland
Mission and Discipleship Council

www.resourcingmission.org.uk

Resourcing Mission is a website from the
Mission & Discipleship Council.

Mission. Worship. Discipleship.

 ## Questions for discussion

1. How would you define the kingdom of God?
2. In what ways do you see the kingdom of God advancing through your congregation?
3. How can elders partake in the advancement of the kingdom of God?

 ## Further resources

· Visit **www.resourcingmission.org.uk** for a range of resources for your congregation.

 Why not try... taking time to reflect on the Lord's Prayer? Begin to imagine what it might look like for the kingdom of God to come here on earth as it is in heaven.

SAINT ANDREW PRESS

www.standrewpress.com

Seonag Mackinnon, Head of Communications in the Church of Scotland, interviews Fiona Buchanan. An elder at Carrick Knowe Parish Church, Edinburgh, Fiona works for the Church and Society Council of the Church of Scotland.

60

SECOND INTERVIEW WITH FIONA BUCHANAN

" I am excited about the people that the Learn initiative will reach.

What is surprising about your role as an elder?

I am 33 and an elder. Eldership at my church is made up of 40 women and men between the ages of 20 and 95 – where else in society do you see that kind of intergenerational working and community being built? I cannot imagine another walk of life in which I would be part of a community of friends - other elders - some of whom are in their twenties and some of whom are older. In fact some of my closest friends from my church community are in their eighties! We are all working together making decisions about our community. A lot of my friends are involved in the church but other friends can be curious about my role and ask me about what I do.

Are you young to be an elder?

I was 28 when I became an elder but my sister Lesley, who was ordained on the same day, was 26. In fact you can become an elder from the age of 18. The word 'elder' makes it sound as though we should all be elderly but people can be wise and have the skills and experience required of an elder at a relatively young age. When our current minister, Rev Fiona Mathieson, arrived she was very keen that younger people should become more involved. We also have many women which doesn't happen everywhere. My sister and I have been in the congregation all our lives so it feels like an extension of the family.

Most challenging aspect of your role?

I serve as Director of Music so I am not a conventional district elder in the sense that I don't have a geographical part of the parish that I look after. This isn't to say that I can't provide this pastoral element of care and nurture but the main way I serve is through music in worship. As an elder I have enjoyed taking on this specific role; it means a great deal to me to serve the church in this way.

What is the day job?

I used to work for Women's Aid which is a national charity that works against domestic abuse. Now half of my working week is at the Church offices in Edinburgh where I am Local Involvement Officer for the Church and Society Council. I might be at a meeting of Glasgow Presbytery about food banks or encouraging people to sign a petition, or finding a speaker for a meeting about fracking or keeping congregations up-to-date with blogs. The rest of my week is spent managing a financial inclusion project for young people at Young Scot, which is the national information and citizenship charity for young people in Scotland.

And in your spare time?

I love running - I like to get out to the hills in the morning, usually before work. I encouraged members of our church to take part in the Edinburgh Marathon Relay to raise funds for St. Columba's Hospice. I also volunteer for Girlguiding Scotland, and travel throughout Europe working for the Ecumenical Youth Council of Europe. I love music, especially alternative folk and blue grass. You might also find me running a music rehearsal, playing piano, organ or cello. Not usually at the same time!

Your hopes for the Church?

I would like to see it continue along the path of being an inclusive and welcoming Church but also be a little more radical, a little less safe. People are interested in the Church and spirituality but not necessarily in the way that we know it. I hope the Church continues to be inclusive. Sometimes it feels as though we have constructed too many barriers and we act as though we are almost scared of the communities we live in and imagine them to be. Showing hospitality and God's love to the people we meet daily and interact with is vital.

Your thoughts on training for elders?

I am excited about the people that the Learn initiative will reach. At the moment about 150 are able to get to conferences and training, but with over 32,000 elders we have more to do! I am excited for this new resource – it allows elders to learn more but also discuss with each other their own ideas too.

Your message to others in the Church?

Look around you. Are there young people in your community who could take on the role of elder? Might you mentor them? Young people can feel quite excluded in the Church. I feel they have to be allowed to take on responsibilities and leadership roles. It makes them more visible and gives them a say in the future of the Church. It is still unusual to have people in their twenties serving as elders. Often, elders are retired. It is not that young people are uninterested - they often just don't have the same availability.

Why does the role of elder matter?

It is good to be involved. I share in key decisions in the church through the Kirk Session meetings throughout the year, play an active part in worship through nurturing peoples' skills and in the community visiting people. My main role has been in relation to music in worship, spending the last 15 years developing this into its current form where we have a much more inclusive attitude to music in worship: more people involved, more varied music reflecting different styles and tastes - and pushing us out of our comfort zones. I think people quite like it once they get over the initial shock. ∎

God of eternity –
through the ages, across continents,
flowering in cultures and singing in a chorus of different tongues,
Your Church in the world,
the Body of Christ,
beloved of God,
faithful and flawed,
beautiful and broken,
honours You today
with its service and thanksgiving.

Jesus said, 'Abide in my love.'
In parish worship,
in private prayers at home, in the community and at the bedside,
in moments of joy and health and spiritual well-being,
in moments of sadness, hurt and insecurity,
the vibrant flame of Resurrection burns
wherever, in peace, we welcome Jesus.
Let Him sit with us,
at one with us, at the centre of the soul.
Christ, listen to our story,
touch and heal us.

God of Truth,
we seek You in the affections of the heart,
in the disciplines of the mind, and
through our shared journeys
learning together,
listening for Your tender silence,
looking for signs of Your Spirit,
in the manifold gifts and blessing of others.

May we feel Your providential hand upon us;
strengthen us in the spiritual virtues of faith, hope and love.
Lead us ever more deeply into the fruits of the Spirit;
may they penetrate our heart and soul:
joy, peace, kindness, gentleness, self-control and humility.
Rid us of all vice:
gluttony, envy, lust, pride, laziness, greed and anger.
May we reflect Your light more truly
that the world will know You.

Amen.

Rev Scott S. McKenna, Mayfield Salisbury Parish Church, www.mayfieldsalisbury.org

AN INTRODUCTION TO
JOHN KNOX

Nikki Macdonald
Minister of Upper Clyde Church, Presbytery of Lanark

Who was John Knox? He is revered by some as a major player in the Protestant Reformation in Scotland, and reviled by others as a kill-joy, bigot, misogynist and the man who made Mary, Queen of Scots, cry.[1] Between hero and villain is the more human Knox – a man of controversy, certainly, but also contrasts and complexity.

Knox was born sometime around 1514 in Giffordgate, Haddington, and after studying at the local school went on to St Andrews University in the late 1520's, although there is no indication that he completed his studies. He then joined the Church, eventually being ordained as a deacon, and then as a priest in the latter part of the 1530's. Although a priest, Knox never had responsibility for a parish, choosing instead to use his knowledge of canon law by working as a notary.

In the early 1540's, back in Haddington, he became a Protestant and changed career; he took up a tutoring post working for two local lairds. Both were Protestant sympathisers and supporters of the Protestant preacher George Wishart. Knox was inspired by Wishart and became a prominent supporter of his work. On 1st March 1546 Wishart was tried for heresy and executed on the same day upon the order of Cardinal David Beaton, Archbishop of St Andrews. The Protestants in St Andrews responded by assassinating Beaton and took control of the castle in May 1546, beginning an 18-month siege.

At Easter 1547, Knox travelled with his pupils to St Andrews and continued tutoring. Increasing pressure was put upon Knox to become a preacher, but he refused until he heard a sermon which ended with a direct challenge. This caused Knox great distress: he promptly burst into tears and hid in his room. After several days, he reluctantly agreed and preached his first sermon in the parish church of Holy Trinity, a polemic affair in which he portrayed the Pope as the Antichrist. This public face of Knox as fiery and prophetic sits in contrast to the private Knox of self-doubt. The French fleet recaptured the castle in July that year, and Knox was sentenced to a spell in the galleys where he remained for 19 months.

After his release, Knox moved to England, ministering at the border town of Berwick in 1549, where he became acquainted with the Bowes family. In gratitude for his pastoral support, Elizabeth Bowes encouraged the relationship between Knox and her daughter, Marjory; they were engaged in 1553. However, in 1551, having been invited to become a royal chaplain to Edward VI, Knox moved to London.

After the death of Edward in 1553 and with the accession of his Catholic sister, Mary Tudor, Knox fled to the continent. In early 1554 he travelled to Geneva and encountered John Calvin before eventually travelling to Frankfurt in November 1554 to minister to English exiles. Knox's time in Frankfurt was brief and stormy as the congregation was divided over theological and liturgical issues. Following a rather frank sermon about the troubles within the congregation, Knox later returned to Berwick.

That winter, he preached to the underground Church in Scotland, protected by powerful Protestant nobles. He was encouraged to take on a leadership role, but, as with his initial call to ministry, he was reluctant to do so. He married Marjory in the spring of 1556, and was in Geneva by the summer, ministering to the English-speaking exiles. Marjory joined him, and his sons, Nathaniel and Eleazer, were born in 1557 and 1558. Knox flourished in Geneva, surrounded by those he loved and trusted, and with Calvin shaping Geneva along Reformed lines to be "that most perfect school of Christ".[2] The lessons he learned in Geneva would be taken back to Scotland, to help with the establishing of Protestantism there.

Knox arrived back in Scotland in 1559 and was immediately drawn into political and religious tensions between the Protestant nobles, Mary of Guise, and the Catholic hierarchy. Preaching in Perth, Knox caused a riot to break out, in which statues and other trappings of Catholicism were destroyed. The movement spread along the Fife coast, assisted by Knox's powerful preaching. St Andrews became a Protestant town and invited Knox to become minister there, which he did briefly. With the death of Mary of Guise, in June 1560, the establishment of Protestantism as the official religion of the realm followed quickly. Knox moved to Edinburgh and became the minister of St Giles. While 1560 was a period of triumph, Knox also faced personal tragedy when Marjory died.

Much has been made of his encounters with Mary, Queen of Scots, who returned from France in August 1561. In fact, they only met four times. Two of these were relatively cordial though robust encounters, but it was the final meeting in June 1563 which ended in Mary's angry tears because of Knox's denunciation of a possible alliance by marriage with Catholic Spain. The following year, 1564, at age 50 Knox married again. His young wife was named Margaret.

Knox's latter years were marked by ill health and depression, and he increasingly considered retirement. He began to remove himself from the centre of the political and religious spheres. In correspondence with friends, Knox noted his disappointment with the way in which he felt that the great hopes of the Reformation had been tarnished by the expediency of political compromise; along with disappointment and melancholy, he now longed for death to take him home to the God he had served. In 1570, he had a slight stroke, which forced him to curtail his activities in order to save his energies for preaching in St Giles. By the autumn of 1572, Knox was seriously ill. He needed to be helped up to his pulpit, and his voice, which had formerly caused people to tremble when he preached, had lost much of its power. He struggled on until 9 November, when he handed over his position as minister. Thereafter, he remained housebound. Over his last remaining weeks, Knox was visited by many friends and supporters, with his young wife nursing him diligently. Knox died on 24 November 1572 and was buried in the graveyard at St Giles. At his funeral, Regent Morton said of Knox:

> *Here lyeth a man who in his life never feared the face of man; who hath beene often threatned with dagge and dagger, but yet hath ended his dayes in peace and honour.*[3] ∎

 Questions for discussion

1. How do you imagine the call to become a Protestant preacher made Knox feel?
2. Have there been times when you have felt God calling you to some particular kind of service, and how have you responded?
3. Knox's style of preaching could be described as powerful, thunderous, even 'hellfire and brimstone'. There are many ways of delivering a sermon: what styles of preaching have you encountered, or used yourself?

 Further reading

- Jane E. A. Dawson, **John Knox**, (Yale: Yale University Press, 2015)
- Gordon Donaldson, **The Scottish Reformation**, (Cambridge: Cambridge University Press, 1960)
- Rosalind K. Marshall, **John Knox**, (Edinburgh: Birlinn, 2000)
- Roderick Graham, **John Knox: man of action**, (Edinburgh: Saint Andrew Press, 2013).

 Why not try... reading the very accessible biography by Rosalind Marshall for a more complete picture of Knox?

1 See Rosalind Marshall, *John Knox*, (Edinburgh: Birlinn, 2000), xii-xiii.
2 John Knox, *The Works of John Knox* vol. 4 ed. David Laing, (Edinburgh), p.240
3 David Calderwood, *The History of the Kirk of Scotland*, vol. 2., ed. T. Thomson and D. Laing, 8 vols., (Edinburgh: Wodrow Society, 1842-9), p.242.

WHAT DOES IT MEAN TO BE "REFORMED"?

Paul Nimmo
Professor in Systematic Theology, University of Aberdeen

The Church of Scotland describes itself as a "Reformed" Church, and is a member of the World Communion of Reformed Churches. Though the term "Reformed" is not regularly used in the life of the Church itself, it offers an important way of describing something of the history and identity of the Church of Scotland.

The term "Reformed" arose in the 16th century, during the early decades of the Protestant Reformation. One of the common allegations of the early Reformers such as Martin Luther and Huldrych Zwingli was that the theology and practice of the medieval Church had departed in significant ways from the teaching of the Bible. In line with their protest against the existing state of affairs, they therefore sought to reform the Church in accordance with the Word of God found in Scripture. In one sense, then, all Protestant Churches are "Reformed", and described themselves as such in the 16th century – indeed, the term "Reformed" itself is simply shorthand for "Reformed according to the Word of God". However, the Reformation not only brought division between the medieval Catholic Church and the emerging Protestant movement; it also brought an almost immediate fragmentation of the Protestant movement into diverse groups, as disputes emerged over how to interpret the Word of God found in Scripture. In the course of the 16th century, a number of groups of Protestant Churches emerged. Among these groups were the Lutheran Churches, principally emerging in Germany and following Martin Luther, and what came to be called "Reformed" Churches, first emerging in the Swiss Confederation and sharing their own theological concerns. In this second sense, the word "Reformed" came to identify "Reformed" churches and views in contrast to those of other Protestants.

> **"...there was an unwavering confession of the unique importance of Scripture...**

Many of the central convictions of "Reformed" Churches were common to all Churches, Reformed, Lutheran, and Catholic alike – such as belief in the Trinity and confession of Jesus Christ as Lord and Saviour. However, in other areas, the Reformed had rather particular views that were differentiated from those of other Churches. A small number of significant Reformed emphases and concerns might be mentioned here. First, there was an unwavering confession of the unique importance of Scripture in serving as the principal rule and guide in all matters relating to the Christian faith. Second, there was a strong emphasis upon God's election of a specific people for the purpose of salvation, and upon God's providence governing the whole of creation to that same end. Third, there was a central insistence that the relationship of the believer to God depended on the faith of the believer and not upon their works. And finally, there was a resolute insistence upon seeing Jesus Christ as being both divine and human, without his divinity and his humanity ever being confused.

Such convictions and their outworkings were expressed in a series of "confessions" and "catechisms" issued by particular Reformed Churches. A number of these were written by significant figures in the Reformed tradition in the 16th century, such as Huldrych Zwingli, Heinrich Bullinger, and – perhaps the most famous – John Calvin. But, in truth, each of these documents speaks for a Church rather than for an individual, declaring the core beliefs of that Church on a range of subjects. The confessions thus contain teaching on theological matters such as the doctrine of God, the act of creation, the fall of humanity, the person of Jesus Christ, justification, sanctification, the Church, and the sacraments. The catechisms, meanwhile, serve as aids to communicate (and memorise) the substance of the confessions, often being employed to teach the young. Neither type of document is intended to replace Scripture; by contrast, all are explicitly subordinate to (and subject to correction by) Scripture.

Important confessions in the life of the Church of Scotland include the Scots Confession of 1560, and the later Westminster Confession adopted in 1647, the latter remaining the Kirk's subordinate standard of faith. Other notable Reformed confessions of the Reformation era include the Heidelberg Catechism of 1563 and the Second Helvetic Confession of 1566. Despite their diverse origins, there exists a high degree of family resemblance across these early documents. In Europe and in North America, there has been far less activity since the 17th century in respect of drafting new confessions; by contrast, the 20th century saw a series of new confessional documents being composed by Churches in Asia and Africa, reflecting the way in which the Reformed family of Churches has extended overseas. And two of the most significant Church documents of the twentieth century were Reformed confessions: the Barmen Declaration of the Confessing Church of Germany of 1934 (in opposition to National Socialism) and the Belhar Confession adopted by the Dutch Reformed Mission Church in South Africa in 1986 (against apartheid).

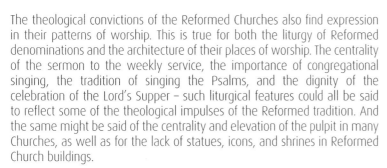

 Questions for discussion

1. What responses do words such as "Reformed", "Calvinist", or "Presbyterian" summon to your mind?
2. Can you think of any ways in which your church demonstrates its "Reformed" connection?
3. Do you think that identifying words such as "Reformed" - or similar terms such as "Anglican" or "Roman Catholic" - have an ongoing place in the Christian life?

 Further reading

· **The Book of Confessions** – a document of the Presbyterian Church of the United States of America at www.pcusa.org/resource/book-confessions.
· G. D. Henderson and James Bulloch, **The Scots Confession of 1560** (Edinburgh: Saint Andrew Press, 2007).

 Why not try ... reading through one of the confessions important for the Church of Scotland – the Scots Confession or the Westminster Confession?
Also, try reading one of the significant confessions of the 20th century – the Barmen Declaration or the Belhar Confession.

The theological convictions of the Reformed Churches also find expression in their patterns of worship. This is true for both the liturgy of Reformed denominations and the architecture of their places of worship. The centrality of the sermon to the weekly service, the importance of congregational singing, the tradition of singing the Psalms, and the dignity of the celebration of the Lord's Supper – such liturgical features could all be said to reflect some of the theological impulses of the Reformed tradition. And the same might be said of the centrality and elevation of the pulpit in many Churches, as well as for the lack of statues, icons, and shrines in Reformed Church buildings.

Two terms are often used as loose synonyms for the term "Reformed". The first is "Calvinist", referring to the person and work of John Calvin, both of which were highly significant for the Reformed tradition. But this descriptor does not do full justice either to the breadth of figures involved in the foundation and development of the Reformed movement, or to the historical and geographical diversity of its Churches. The second is "Presbyterian", referring to one possible pattern of Church government which has been highly dominant within the Reformed tradition in general and Scotland in particular. Yet there is no necessary link between Reformed theology and Presbyterian government; indeed, Reformed Churches are often congregational and occasionally episcopal in their mode of organisation. For these reasons, the term "Reformed" is to be preferred in most Church discourse.

In the centuries since the Reformation, Reformed Churches have developed in a series of highly diverse and rapidly changing contexts. The basic insights and core convictions of the original Reformed confessions and theologians have been carried forward in various ways. For many people in Reformed Churches, the confessions remain not just important but even essential to a proper understanding of the Christian faith in light of Scripture, and therefore their letter remains as binding and effective as it was in the 16th century. For other people in Reformed Churches, the confessions set forth a series of core theological affirmations and instincts that by the power of the Spirit seek and find fresh expression in different ages, thereby witnessing to the ongoing vitality of the work of theology. Many of the most influential theologians in the later years of the Reformed tradition – such as Jonathan Edwards, Friedrich Schleiermacher, Herman Bavinck, Karl Barth, and Thomas Torrance – have engaged in diverse ways with the underlying questions of continuity and development. And in the same vein, the Reformed Churches have been at or near the centre of many of the most significant ecumenical impulses and events of the 20th century. Ultimately, for all parties in the Reformed tradition, the oft-cited Reformed statement that "the Church is reformed and always (in need of) being reformed according to the Word of God" is held to have ongoing relevance and significance. ■

THE WESTMINSTER CONFESSION - PAST AND PRESENT

Paul Nimmo
Professor in Systematic Theology, University of Aberdeen

The Westminster Confession is the "principal subordinate standard" of the Church of Scotland, meaning that it serves as the historically agreed expression of the Church's faith, which gives assistance in the correct interpretation of the Scriptures. Yet the significance ascribed to it and the practices related to it have seen considerable development and variance over the centuries since its first approval.

Historically, the Confession was the product of the Westminster Assembly, a gathering of ministers and laymen called to meet by the English Parliament in 1643. Among the purposes of this Assembly were to reform the liturgy and organisation of the Church of England, to clarify its theological position, and to promote Church unity with the Church of Scotland. To this end, and with the aid of a small but influential advisory group of delegates from the Church of Scotland, the Assembly over the ensuing years produced a series of documents: "The Directory of Public Worship" setting out a liturgy, "The Form of Church Government" setting out a polity, and "The Westminster Confession" (together with a Larger and a Shorter Catechism) setting out a theological position. As political and religious alignments in England shifted over the course of the Civil War, none of the Assembly's documents ever gained significant status there. In Scotland, however, the Westminster Confession – often simply referred to

> " **The Confession thus came to have an authority and importance second only to Scripture itself.**

as "the Confession" – was approved by the General Assembly of the Church of Scotland in 1647. By the early 18th century, it was necessary for all its ministers and elders to subscribe to a declaration that they believed the whole doctrine contained in the Confession, and would assert, maintain, and defend it. The Confession thus came to have an authority and importance second only to Scripture itself.

The Confession, like other Reformed confessions, provides a statement of the Christian faith of the original writers (and its subsequent subscribers) in relation to a broad array of theological topics. It is organised into 33 chapters of different lengths, moving from its view of Scripture, God and the Trinity through the doctrines of creation, providence, fall, redemption, the Christian life, and the Church to its understanding of last things. Every section of the Confession is accompanied by proof-texts from Scripture, in an effort to demonstrate its orthodoxy and reliability. Indeed, given its high view of the authority of Scripture, the Confession implicitly recognises its own subordination to Scripture and thus that it is provisional and fallible.

Throughout, the substance of the Confession is particularly indebted to the theology of John Calvin, and exhibits many of the same emphases as his work. Thus there is in the Confession a clear assertion that God is absolutely sovereign, that Christ alone is our Mediator, and that redemption brings gracious benefits to the believer. Also following Calvin, it confesses that, in eternity, God chooses some people for salvation and others for damnation; moreover, and arguably following Calvin, it correspondingly limits the benefits of the work of Jesus Christ to those in the former, elect group. In other ways, however, the Confession moves beyond Calvin himself and draws on certain later trajectories in Reformed theology. This is particularly evident in its understanding of the relationship between God and humanity (the Confession sets forth an original "covenant of works" between God and Adam, which is fulfilled by means of the "covenant of grace" between God and humanity in Jesus Christ).

In the course of its history, there have been a number of challenges to the position of the Westminster Confession. Some of these challenges have come from outwith: for example, in the later years of the 17th century, the Confession had no official status in the Church of Scotland at all, albeit it remained in practice a guide to its faith. But most of these challenges have come from within. In the mid-18th century, for example, many in the Moderate party in the Church of Scotland decried the value of the Confession. This was an era in which both the form and the content of Christian confessions were subject to intense scrutiny and vigorous criticism, on grounds not only of Enlightenment rationalism but also of theological correctness. Again in the mid-19th century, subscription to the Confession became increasingly difficult for a significant number of Church figures. This was a time of growing historical awareness and scientific knowledge, a time in which fresh perceptions of the nature of humanity

and the desirability of tolerance were enlivened by the experience of Christian mission. In the latter years of the century, there were a number of heresy trials in the Reformed Churches of Scotland, as the theology of the Confession found itself left behind in some quarters. More recently, in 1986, the General Assembly declared that it no longer affirmed certain clauses of the Confession which denounced Roman Catholic Church practices and persons, and that it therefore did not require office-bearers to believe them. And more broadly, a series of late 20th–century Reformed theologians expressed grave reservations about some of the theology contained in the Confession, criticising it for being rather legalistic in its view, and for offering insufficient descriptions of the gracious love of God, of the work of the Holy Spirit, and of the missionary task of the Church.

The situation in the current day reflects something of the effect of such controversies. As things stand, ministers and elders in the Church of Scotland are read the following statement as part of their service of ordination:

> The Church of Scotland holds as its subordinate standard the Westminster Confession of Faith, recognising liberty of opinion on such points of doctrine as do not enter into the substance of the Faith, and claiming the right, in dependence on the promised guidance of the Holy Spirit, to formulate, interpret, or modify its subordinate standards always in agreement with the Word of God and the fundamental doctrines of the Christian Faith contained in the said Confession, of which agreement the Church itself shall be sole judge.

The candidate for ordination is then asked to respond to a question and to subscribe to a statement such that they affirm that they "believe the fundamental doctrines of the Christian faith contained in the Confession of Faith of this Church".

This procedure results in a certain ambiguity. On the one hand, it upholds the historic position that the Westminster Confession is the "subordinate standard" of the Church of Scotland, though it explicitly acknowledges that the Confession may be subject to modification, "always in agreement with the Word of God". On the other hand, it recognises that individuals may exercise "liberty of opinion" on points of doctrine not entering "into the substance of the faith", i.e. not entering upon "the fundamental doctrines of the Christian Faith". The trouble is, of course, that "the substance" and "the fundamental doctrines" of the faith are nowhere defined. An informed and energetic attempt on the part of the Panel on Doctrine in the 1970's to bring greater clarity to this issue did not make any significant progress in the General Assembly.

This situation leads to the presence of a wide spectrum of opinion regarding the Westminster Confession within the Church of Scotland today. Three alternative views might be noted here. For some, the Confession sets forth a definitive expression of the faith of the Kirk, offering a perennially valid marker of its identity and its orthodoxy. It therefore deserves greater attention and firmer subscription. For others, the Confession represents a significant document in the development of Reformed theology, and one worthy of ongoing reception as part of theological reflection today. It thus remains important but is not beyond criticism and correction. Yet others view the Confession as highly anachronistic and/or simply erroneous in its theological views. It is correspondingly to be viewed as broadly irrelevant for the Church today.

It is certainly true that the existing imprecision concerning the extent to which ministers and elders may or may not subscribe to the Westminster Confession is not a wholly satisfactory situation, lacking in both clarity and transparency. However, given the wide array of theological views in the Church of Scotland in general, let alone on the Confession in particular, perhaps this imprecision is in truth a rather happy affair, facilitating a legitimate diversity within the sphere of the Christian Church. ∎

Questions for discussion

1. What sort of beliefs would you consider to be "the substance of the faith"?
2. Do you think "the substance of the faith" is something that changes over time?
3. What role do you think historic documents should have in today's Church?

Further reading

- The Westminster Confession of Faith – available online at **www.churchofscotland.org.uk/about_us/our_faith/westminster_confession_of_faith**
- Alasdair I. C. Heron (ed.), **The Westminster Confession in the Church Today** (Edinburgh: Saint Andrew Press, 1982).

 Why not try... reading some of the Westminster Confession? Also, try reading some of the Westminster Larger and Shorter Catechisms.

THE COURTS OF THE KIRK

Marjory MacLean

Minister of Abernyte L.W. Inchture & Kinnaird L.W. Longforgan, Presbytery of Dundee

In the Church of Scotland the courts of the Church – General Assembly, Presbyteries and Kirk Sessions – set the policy and supervise the governance of our denomination. Only the courts of the Church do this. Contrast the Church of Scotland with Churches that have a different kind of governance. We do not place policy-formation in the hands of any individual (e.g. bishops, archbishops or deans), nor do we give it to any other corporate body (e.g. synods, chapters or conferences).

Next, contrast the courts of our Church with the other elements of governance we have: Councils at national level, committees at all levels, and other kinds of task groups and working groups that are known by all sorts of different names. All of these confine themselves to implementing the policy of the relevant court, bringing to the parent body any decisions that constitute policy-formation. So a Presbytery's Education Committee, for example, might nurture and support its candidates in training for ministry; but it would require the Presbytery as a whole to take the initial decision to nominate that person as a candidate. If a decision is "strategic" it goes to the court, and if it is "executive" it is kept in the committee. And if there's any doubt or dispute as to which of those it is, it is taken to the court to be on the safe side.

That principle is hardest to achieve at General Assembly level, simply because the Assembly meets only for a week each May, while its executive committees (such as the Councils of the Church) work all year round. Unavoidably, as unexpected questions and unpredictable problems come up during the year, those bodies will have to make decisions that come close to creating policy. This is done only when it cannot be avoided; it cannot relate to really high-level matters like doctrine; and the policy should always then be ratified by the next General Assembly. Presbyteries and Kirk Sessions meet more regularly: therefore, committees of these courts can more frequently refer policy-making decisions to them.

There are three courts, then, and they connect to each other in several ways, depending on the kind of work they are doing. Like any legal system, the Church of Scotland sometimes makes policy and rules (what you might call a legislative function), sometimes concentrates on implementing that policy (an executive function), and sometimes sorts out disputes and disagreements (a judicial function), and the civil law gives the Church of Scotland a great deal of freedom to do that without external legal interference.

In the legislative function, think of a cascade model, where a law or decision of the General Assembly binds everyone, a decision of a Presbytery binds only the congregations of that Presbytery, and a decision of a Kirk Session cannot be inconsistent with the higher-order rules of the "superior" courts.

In the executive function, think more of a flat structure of concentric circles with the congregation in the middle: the executive agencies of the Assembly and Presbyteries are largely devoted to supporting and resourcing the local congregation in its work, and are there to help, not so much to regulate.

In the judicial function, think of a vertical structure of binding decisions, one court strictly above another. However, bear in mind that mediation and reconciliation systems are developing enormously in the Church of Scotland, and improving our style of dispute resolution year on year.

As an elder you may serve on Presbytery or in the General Assembly. Wherever you serve, remember that is where spiritual governance is formally exercised. Remember too, though, that spiritual leadership may be exercised anywhere and everywhere in the Kirk's life and work. ∎

 Questions for discussion

1. What sorts of issues would count as the kind of spiritual and strategic decisions that belong to the courts of the Church of Scotland?
2. What sorts of questions properly belong to the General Assembly to decide?
3. And can you think of examples of issues that are best decided by your local Presbytery?

 Further reading

· Marjory MacLean (ed.), **The Legal Systems of Scottish Churches**, (Dundee: University Press, 2010).
· Marjory MacLean, **Crown Rights of the Redeemer: the spiritual freedom of the Church of Scotland**, (Edinburgh: Saint Andrew Press, 2009).

 Why not try... attending a meeting of your local Presbytery, or a session of the General Assembly in May?

WHAT IS A KIRK SESSION?

Marjory MacLean

Minister of Abernyte L.W. Inchture & Kinnaird L.W. Longforgan, Presbytery of Dundee

The Kirk Session is the lowest of the three courts, and governs the life of a congregation. It is the body that makes policy relating to matters spiritual – areas like worship, mission, education, ecumenical work and so on.

There's one element of our governance that causes some doubt in relation to this, and that's the Congregational Board, Deacons' Court or Committee of Management. If your congregation has none of these, then decisions relating to property, finance and stewardship are handled by the Kirk Session and its committees, in addition to more obviously "spiritual" matters. In all other cases your congregation will have one of those three bodies. The safest way to proceed is to regard that body as if it were a committee of the Kirk Session (though, constitutionally, it is a separate body) i.e. a body referring all strategic decisions, and definitely all decisions that touch on spiritual matters like worship resources and the sanctuary, to the Kirk Session; and the Kirk Session for its part should take the Board's (or equivalent) advice on matters of property, finance and stewardship. Some decisions require the formal consent of both Session and Board (or equivalent) and these should clearly be made by both bodies separately, each focusing on its particular remit – the Kirk Session looking at the strategic spiritual question, and the Board (or equivalent) looking at the more technical aspect.

People often associate the earliest Kirk Sessions and Presbyteries with prayer and study; and many Kirk Sessions rightly emulate that, conducting Bible studies or other spiritual exercises in the course of meetings. But the Kirk Session is a legal entity, and that should not be overlooked, or great confusion may follow.

The Session should meet formally only as that Kirk Session. In law there is no such thing as a 'joint' meeting, either with a different kind of body (Board, Deacons' Court, etc), or with another Kirk Session; in many cases it would be difficult to know what decisions the members of the Session had made and by what majority. By all means, it is possible to have an informal conference of several decision-making bodies together (for example, the Kirk Sessions in a linkage, meeting to talk through issues of common concern); but then it is important to take the decisions separately in each Kirk Session so that the policy is properly made and recorded in minutes.

Finally, the Kirk Session's moderator is the minister or interim moderator of the charge, who carries that responsibility between meetings, even if he or she for any reason has appointed someone else to chair the meeting – and there are regulations enabling that to happen in certain prescribed circumstances.

Questions of procedure, legal responsibility and trusteeship are hugely important, and beyond the scope of this article. It is absolutely vital that all new elders – who as such are charity trustees for civil law purposes – should read the materials available on the Church of Scotland's website (see below). In practice, you will learn most by observation, and by asking questions of the Session Clerk, often a very experienced elder who knows how it all works. ∎

 Questions for discussion

1. What form of constitution does your congregation have: Unitary (i.e. Kirk Session only), Model (Congregational Board), Deacons' Court or Committee of Management?
2. Can you think of the sort of project that would require to be considered first by the financial court, but then by the Kirk Session because it had a spiritual element to it?

 Further reading

- For a full list of elders' resources please see **www.churchofscotland.org.uk/learn** - such as Notes on the Constitutions of the Church of Scotland and a link to the Law Department's Law Circulars.

 Why not try… reading the Kirk Session's minutes for the last three years or so, and note what pieces of business are transacted at certain times of the year (e.g. when the accounts are adopted, when the representative elder to the Presbytery is elected, when the congregational roll is adjusted)?

THE SPIRITUAL OFFICE OF THE ELDER

Gordon Kennedy

Minister of Craiglockhart Church, Presbytery of Edinburgh; Trustee of Rutherford House

The apostle Peter writes of the Church,

> LIKE LIVING STONES, LET YOURSELVES BE BUILT INTO A SPIRITUAL HOUSE, TO BE A HOLY PRIESTHOOD, TO OFFER SPIRITUAL SACRIFICES ACCECTABLE TO GOD THROUGH JESUS CHRIST. (1 PETER 2.5)

We know that it is the purpose of God for all God's people to be spiritual people, to become this spiritual house and offer spiritual sacrifices to God. And yet, as a gift to God's Church God gives some to be elders, to fulfil a spiritual role in the life of the Church, serving both God and the people of God. It is this spiritual office or role of the elder that is our focus.

Let's clarify what we mean by "spiritual" in this article. We are using the word, as the New Testament does, to describe the difference between that which is carried out in the power and presence of the Holy Spirit of God and that which is not. The apostle Paul prays for the Christians in Colossae,

> FOR THIS REASON, SINCE THE DAY WE HEARD IT, WE HAVE NOT CEASED PRAYING FOR YOU AND ASKING THAT YOU MAY BE FILLED WITH THE KNOWLEDGE OF GOD'S WILL IN ALL SPIRITUAL WISDOM AND UNDERSTANDING (COLOSSIANS 1.9)

There is a wisdom and understanding which is not spiritual, which is not guided or informed by the Spirit of God. In contrast to this there is a spiritual wisdom, God's own Spirit at work within God's people making us wise in the things of God. Elders in the Church exercise a spiritual office. This tells us that the work of an elder is to be empowered and inspired by God's Spirit. There are many tasks undertaken by elders: attending meetings, visiting, praying, leading worship, and serving on committees or working groups. We could do all this in our own strength or in a human wisdom and not fulfil our role as elders. However, since our work is a spiritual work we seek to live and serve as elders in a way that is filled with the presence and power of the Holy Spirit.

How can we know the presence and power of the Holy Spirit guiding us in our serving in the spiritual office of the elder? In this short article, let me mention just two key themes in answer to this question.

First, let's consider the role of growing in God's Word. In Psalm 1 we read of the person who is blessed by the Lord,

> BUT THEIR DELIGHT IS IN THE LAW OF THE LORD,
> AND ON HIS LAW THEY MEDITATE DAY AND NIGHT
> THEY ARE LIKE TREES
> PLANTED BY STREAMS OF WATER,
> WHICH YIELD THEIR FRUIT IN ITS SEASON,
> AND THEIR LEAVES DO NOT WITHER.
> IN ALL THAT THEY DO, THEY PROSPER.
> (PSALM 1.2-3)

The God who gives us the Holy Spirit is a living and active God speaking to us today. The Lord Jesus is made known to us as the Word of God. When the Holy Spirit is poured out upon God's people, they speak, "about God's deeds of power" (Acts 2.11). God has given us God's Word written down in the pages of the Holy Scriptures. If we would serve God in a spiritual office, we will grow in this service as we grow in God's Word. There is no substitute for the reading of God's Word. If that tree did not drink daily from the life-giving water it would soon wither and be fruitless. As we daily drink the life-giving Word of our living God so we learn of God and grow more like Christ. Through God's Word we learn of God's love for us, God's mission in the world, and God's purposes for the Church. God's Word is the water from which we draw our life, and our spiritual service can only be strong and healthy as we read God's Word.

Secondly, let's consider the role of prayer within our spiritual role.

> HE WAS PRAYING IN A CERTAIN PLACE,
> AND AFTER HE HAD FINISHED, ONE OF HIS
> DISCIPLES SAID TO HIM, "LORD, TEACH US
> TO PRAY, AS JOHN TAUGHT HIS DISCIPLES."
> (LUKE 11.1)

Spiritual people are praying people. Elders who hold a spiritual office must be praying people. And yet, however long we have been a disciple of the Lord Jesus we feel as though we are just beginning in prayer. Be encouraged to hear those first disciples asking their Lord and our Lord, "Teach us to pray".

When we pray we are saying that we can't do this on our own: we are trusting the Lord to whom we pray. When we pray we approach the Scriptures in that attitude of dependence and humility as we ask the Lord who speaks the words of Scripture to us to guide us in reading and understanding them. Every part of our Christian living and eldership service is strengthened by prayer. John Bunyan writes, "You can do more than pray, after you have prayed, but you cannot do more than pray until you have prayed."

In our prayers we ask for God to be at work through our service. Do not hesitate to ask, the Lord Jesus taught us: "Ask and it will be given to you" (Luke 11.9). In our prayers we still our hearts to enjoy the presence of our God and to know God as our Father and Lord.

We serve as elders in this spiritual office through dedication to prayer and reading of the Scriptures. This is how we learn to depend on the Holy Spirit, and let God's love and grace shine through all that we do. May this be our chief desire in serving God and his Church in the office of the elder. ∎

Questions for discussion

1. Are there situations in which you find it difficult to trust God? How might you learn to trust God more?
2. What parts of Scripture do you find encouraging? What parts do you find challenging? How can you develop your reading of the Scriptures?
3. Do you find it easy to pray? How might you develop prayer within your role as an elder?

Further Reading:

- Gordon D. Fee and Douglas Stuart **How to Read the Bible for All Its Worth** (Grand Rapids, MI: Zondervan: 2003)
- John Stott, **Understanding the Bible**, revised edition (Milton Keynes: Scripture Union, 2003)
- Eric J. Alexander, **Prayer: a biblical perspective** (Edinburgh: The Banner of Truth Trust, 2012)
- Eugene H. Peterson, **Answering God: learning to pray from the Psalms** (London: Harper Collins, 1989)

For eldership resources and support visit Rutherford House at **www.rutherfordhouse.org.uk**

Why not try... choosing a book of the Bible and reading a chapter every day? Make notes about your reactions and thoughts. Consider what God might be saying to you through your reading.

AN INTRODUCTION TO CHURCH DISCIPLINE

Nikki Macdonald

Minister of Upper Clyde Church, Presbytery of Lanark

Discipline is a key marker of the Church of Scotland and features in the declaration and affirmation of the elder at ordination. But what does it mean? Sketching some of its history will help answer this question.

On 17th August 1560, an Act of Parliament approved what is now known as *The Scots Confession of Faith*. The aim of the Confession was to "notify unto the world the sum of that doctrine" professed by Protestants.[1] Further, it was a call to holy conduct, acting as both catechism and compass, instructing the nation as it navigated the stormy sea of sin. Underpinned by the support of the Reformation Parliament, the Church aimed to bring every aspect of Scottish life under its control. Through such regulation of people's lives, it was hoped that the Church would enable the call to holy conduct to be realised through the creation of a holy nation.[2] By a stroke of the pen, the law of God and the law of the land were to be united in common purpose, working together for the glory of God to the blessing of the people.

Scottish reformers viewed Scotland as a new Israel, bound, like ancient Israel before it, in a covenantal relationship with God. This special relationship was accompanied by a responsibility to obey God's commands. Viewed in parallel with the experience of Israel, the establishment of Church discipline was deemed to be essential in order for survival: obedience brought God's blessing, while disobedience brought potential disaster, such as crop failure, flood, or plague. In order to ensure God's blessing, the support of civil government was essential; the civil sword of criminal law working alongside the ecclesial sword of discipline was what would give Church discipline its sharpness.

The primary purpose of discipline was to restore relationships, divine and human; it was about reconciliation. In order to reconcile, faults had to be acknowledged, confessed, and repented. Only then could the offence be forgiven and the relationship restored. The biblical text that provided the template for reconciling neighbours was Matthew 18.15-18, which moved from private to public reconciliation depending upon what reformers, such as John Knox, referred to as the 'obstinacy' of the offender.

The visibility of the Church played an important part within the need to maintain discipline. In a society which placed a great deal in reputation and personal honour, Protestant reformers had a dim view of those whose offences were in the public domain. Such offenders brought dishonour upon God's name and upon the reputation of the community of the godly. Obvious misbehaviour undermined the Protestant cause: having judged the Catholic Church and found it wanting, it was imperative that Protestants kept their own house in order.

While the backing of government enabled discipline to be an effective behavioural corrective, what strengthened it further was that discipline was mostly performed at local level by the Kirk Session. In this, elders were crucial in maintaining Church discipline through keeping a watch on their neighbours. When not listening to disciplinary cases in Session, elders were out in the parish. On Sunday mornings, elders would walk around the village or town in order to catch Sabbath-breakers, and in the weeks prior to communion, they would visit people in their districts to undertake communion examinations. In order to receive communion, parishioners were tested on their knowledge of the faith. They were expected to be

able to recite the Ten Commandments, the Lord's Prayer, the Creed, and in some cases of suspected Catholicism, to demonstrate a doctrinal understanding of communion itself.

Church discipline also demonstrated a particular understanding of sin. As the physical body needed to be healthy, so too did the soul. Sin was seen as an illness of the soul which needed the spiritual medicine of discipline to assist its healing as well as to prevent the spread of infection to the wider body of Christ. The variety of remedies available in the disciplinary medicine cabinet ranged from simple, private confession through to the uttermost remedy, excommunication. Excommunication was used rarely, and was often lengthy, reflecting Protestant criticisms that in previous practice it had been used too frequently and too swiftly.[3]

The Protestant Church in Scotland had always attempted to manage the human condition, which it perceived to be flawed and sinful. Accordingly, the achievement of the godly commonwealth required not only prayer but also the disciplined behaviour of its citizens, remembering that even the community of the elect was comprised of repentant sinners. Given the Scots Confession's call to holy conduct, Church discipline gave a practical shape and structure to living in obedience to God and provided a process of restoration for those who had fallen. It was a foundational tool in the reformers' attempts to demonstrate to the world a little glimpse of the kingdom of heaven on earth. ■

1. The Records of the Parliaments of Scotland to 1707, eds. K.M. Brown et al., (St Andrews, 2007-2012), A1560/8/3. http://www.rps.ac.uk. Date accessed: 13 September 2014.
2. See Timothy George, *Theology of the Reformers* (Nashville, Tenn.: Broadman Press, 1988), p.236.
3. At the very minimum, the process of excommunicating an offender took nine weeks, and at each step of the process, the offender was given the opportunity to make their repentance. Should they choose to repent, the process of excommunication was effectively stopped.

 ## Questions for discussion

1. What was the role of the elder in maintaining Church discipline?
2. How does this contrast with the role of the elder now?
3. The call to holy conduct has been an important aspect of church life from its very beginning. Reflect on your own understanding of what holy living is in 21st-century Scotland.

Further reading

- Philip Benedict, **Christ's Churches Purely Reformed: a social history of Calvinism**, (New Haven [Conn.]: Yale University Press, 2002)
- Jane E. A. Dawson, **"Discipline and the Making of a Protestant Scotland."** in *Worship and Liturgy in Context: Studies and Case Studies in Theology and Practice*, edited by Duncan B. Forrester and D. Gay, 123-136. (London: SCM, 2009)
- Jane E. A. Dawson, "Ane Perfyt Reformed Kyrk", in **Humanism and Reform: the Church in Europe, England, and Scotland, 1400-1643**, ed. James Kirk (Oxford: Blackwell Publishers, 1991)
- G. D. Henderson and James Bulloch, **The Scots Confession of 1560** (Edinburgh: Saint Andrew Press, 2007).

 Why not try... working through the first official statement of the Protestant faith in Scotland: the Scots Confession of the Faith? Summarise the key points: what was it trying to teach the early Scottish Protestants about their faith?

THE ELDER AND THE MINISTER

Colin Sinclair

Minister of Palmerston Place, Presbytery of Edinburgh;
Convener of Mission and Discipleship Council

Congregation leadership is a collegiate responsibility given to the Kirk Session, not simply to the minister. The Kirk Session comprises of the minister - the "teaching elder" - and the "ruling elders". There may also be an Ordained Local Minister or a deacon.

Everyone in a Kirk Session has been ordained to their ministry, and as a result, accepts the privileges and responsibilities of office. Elders are expected to be active in the life of the congregation and have a key responsibility in regular attendance at Kirk Session meetings. Under OSCR regulations, elders at Session are responsible for decisions, whether present or not. Some elders, while remaining elders, but no longer being able to attend Kirk Session meetings, retire from Session, freeing them from any legal responsibility for decisions made. At Session, a moderator, commonly the minister, ensures that business is conducted properly. All Kirk Session meetings are open, so, unless for special business, any member can attend, although they come as observers and cannot speak or vote. The Session works best when elders are regularly informed of the work of both Presbytery and the General Assembly. This reflects our Church structure, plus ensures Kirk Sessions are aware of resources provision.

Kirk Sessions work effectively when there are strong and trusting relationships. Much of the time in a Kirk Session is rightly spent on business matters; therefore, it can be invaluable to an eldership team to spend time together outside of the Kirk Session agenda. These informal meetings can be the bedrock of a good team. Depending on the parish, elders may meet each other regularly in the course of the week. Where, however, the congregation is scattered, then more intentional effort is needed to ensure friendships are built that will allow for robust and healthy discussion.

Session meetings in my experience last about an hour and a half. To make the best use of that meeting takes prayer and preparation. Prayer for the Session is an important part of any regular Church prayer meeting. Preparation involves sitting down with the clerk or, if appropriate, a coordinating team involving the minister, Session Clerk, treasurer, and other key leaders. This group can draw up the agenda, identify issues, do basic "housekeeping" and see what information is needed so elders can reach decisions. Nothing is more frustrating than a decision deferred because of inadequate preparation. The agenda and papers should go out over a week before the Session to allow everyone time to read and reflect and prepare for the meeting.

Questions for discussion

1. In what ways could you prepare better for Session meetings to use the time more effectively?
2. In the coming year how might your Kirk Session set aside time to consider the future direction, and would outside help make a difference?
3. In what ways can you ensure the Kirk Session is kept informed of what is happening within the Church of Scotland?

Why not try... making a list of things that you would like to be giving God thanks for in five years? Then work out some of the first steps that you would take to get there.

If people know the meeting will have a clear time limit (for example, 90 minutes), a well-planned agenda, and sufficient backing information, then they will come prepared to work hard to give the leadership the congregation needs. It can be helpful to avoid "any other business" at the end of a Kirk Session when people are tired. Instead, at the start of the session include an item for "notice of business" in which matters outwith the agenda can be raised and assessed as to whether they fit within the existing items, or require discussion at the end, or are best dealt with in a subsequent Kirk Session.

It might be worth considering including one item for wider discussion that focuses on the "bigger picture" of the church. This can encourage broad leadership thought within the Kirk Session and avoid a simplistic management model.

The provision of leadership by the Kirk Session is a spiritual responsibility that demands the best from us, makes us dependent on God and can give great satisfaction. ■

HIS DISCIPLES REMEMBERED THAT IT WAS WRITTEN, "ZEAL FOR YOUR HOUSE WILL CONSUME ME."

John 2:17

God of cosmos and community,
whose love births diversity and difference,
we praise You
that our fulfilment and completion
are found on the paths of reconciliation and justice.

In serving one another,
we ask that the mind of Christ be in us:
unselfishness, self-sacrifice, compassion and tenderness.
In all circumstances,
with Jesus at our side,
may we move from hostility to hospitality,
from fear to love,
from loneliness to spiritual solitude, and
from exclusion to inclusion.

May our hearts embrace our sisters and brothers.
Like the Trinity,
may we draw the circle wide
and welcome to Christ's Table
every searching soul,
where friend and stranger are one:
belonging.

In caring,
may we listen with the heart,
enter one another's pain and joy,
attend to the inner life,
extend the dimensions of the soul,
and while in this world,
keep our eyes fixed on Jesus,
and anchored to the One
who, beyond the horizons, is in all things,
the One in whom all things are.

Amen.

Rev Scott S. McKenna, Mayfield Salisbury Parish Church, www.mayfieldsalisbury.org

THE ELDER AND PUBLIC WORSHIP

Dan Carmichael

Minister of Lenzie Union Church, Presbytery of Glasgow;
Vice-Convener of Mission and Discipleship Council

Public worship was the setting for John Henry Lorimer's painting, *The Ordination of Elders in a Scottish Kirk* and depicts some aspects of an elder's role in worship. The artist captures the moment when the white-haired minister with an open Bible in front of him raised his wrinkled hands in prayer over the group of elders gathered with him around the communion table. These newly ordained elders would join the Session in ensuring that worship took place in the parish to the glory of God, but also for the sake of the only two members of the congregation the artist included: a young girl and an elderly woman. However, these elders in the painting were also individuals, joining in public worship themselves and having their own individual responsibilities within the congregation.

There is a huge variety of roles that individual elders take on in public worship, and we can picture a few of them. At the heavy oak door of a historic parish church or at the glass door of a community centre, elders are among the group welcoming people to worship. At a kitchen table, with a Bible and a laptop, an elder is preparing for the talk they are to give at the Souper Sunday service. In a living-room, a group of elders are meeting to plan a service in three weeks' time; it will be the sixth service they will have led since their minister retired. In a church hall, elders have come to the point in the Kirk Session meeting where they are to discuss the possibility of holding an additional service at a different time with a different style of music.

As well as the roles they take on in public worship, elders often hear what other people think of worship through being a district elder or simply through being a part of the congregation. A few hours visiting in a district can make an elder's head spin with thoughts about worship. A visit to an elderly couple might mean listening to criticism of new music and too many all-age services, while a visit to a busy mum might mean listening to her worries that her daughter has stopped going to church because there isn't enough new music. And in both houses there is the expectation that the elder can do something about it!

What happens during a service of public worship is largely the sole responsibility of the minister, who is answerable to the Presbytery rather than to the Kirk Session. However, Kirk Sessions have a number of wide ranging responsibilities which can have a considerable impact on worship and it might be helpful to briefly state these responsibilities and what the law of the Church of Scotland outlines.

1. Place of worship. All Kirk Sessions have an important role in deciding on any alterations to the interior of church buildings. (see www.resourcingmission.org.uk/carta)
2. Times of worship. The Kirk Session "shall determine the hours of public worship and the times of dispensing the Lord's Supper". (Act III, 2000 section 37(10))
3. Appointment of those who lead praise. "The Kirk Session shall appoint the organist or precentor." (Act III, 2000 section 37(7))
4. Leadership of worship. "The occasional conduct of public worship by an elder or elders of the congregation" was added to the list of those eligible to conduct public worship in 2000. (Act II, 2000 section 27)

These areas of responsibility are in addition to the responsibility of care for worship which is implicit in the vow taken at ordination to uphold the worship of "this Church", as well as to "seek the unity and peace of this Church".

The clearly defined responsibilities which the Kirk Session has towards public worship could be partly summed up in the role of a host: the Session makes sure the setting is right, the Session agrees on the time, and the Session ensures that there are musicians available to lead the congregation in praising God.

The role of host in worship is vital and will have a critical impact on worship. If Kirk Sessions can be seen in some way as a host within public worship then the Session will be looking in all things to welcome the presence of God and the presence of others. John's Gospel records Mary, Martha and Lazarus acting as hosts for Jesus and the disciples before his arrival in Jerusalem. As they welcomed them the hosts learned that they could not please everyone at once, and Mary's extravagant anointing of Jesus' feet (John 12.1-7) as an act of worship sent Judas Iscariot into a rage! Like those early church hosts in Bethany, Kirk Sessions often find that they cannot please everyone.

Shortly after that meal at Bethany the disciple Philip found himself acting as the host to Greek visitors who had come to Jerusalem to worship at the time of the Passover. Their question to the host was a simple one: "Sir, we want to see Jesus." (John 12.21) This suggests that the role of host in public worship may be to prepare for Christ to be seen and to prepare others to see Christ.

The role of the Kirk Session may therefore be partly one of ensuring that there is nothing for which it is responsible that could hinder others from encountering Christ in public worship. The responsibility of the Session as host is to focus its discussions on Christ and on the needs of the parish they serve rather than the individual likes and dislikes of elders. Acting as a host in public worship may lead Kirk Sessions and elders into unexpected territory, but if we have the guidance of the Holy Spirit then Session meetings like public worship ought never to be predictable! ∎

 Questions for discussion

1. Does the place where you worship help to prepare newcomers to encounter Christ in public worship? Are there any changes that could be made to improve its witness to Christ?

   (Note: The 2014 General Assembly instructed the Committee on Church Art and Architecture (CARTA) "in support of the General Trustees, to take on a more pro-active role within Presbyteries in stimulating and supporting congregations to think creatively about how their buildings might be adapted for worship and witness in the 21st century".)

2. Are the times when your congregation meets for public worship convenient for the needs of your parish now?
3. What do you find helpful about public worship in your congregation? Do newcomers find the same thing helpful too?

 Why not try... the next time you are at public worship, think of one of your friends who does not come to church and try to imagine what they would think of the service?

 the role of host in public worship may be to prepare for Christ to be seen and to prepare others to see Christ.

SERVING THE SACRAMENTS

Derek Browning

Minister of Morningside Parish Church, Presbytery of Edinburgh;
Convener of Assembly Arrangements Committee

Robert Bruce, Minister of St Giles in 1589 wrote:

"There is nothing in this world, nor out of the world, more to be craved and sought of every one of you, than to be conjoined, and once for all made one with the God of glory, Christ Jesus...It is brought about by means of the word and preaching of the Gospel; and it is brought about by means of the sacraments, and ministration thereof. The word leads us to Christ by the ear; the sacraments lead us to Christ by the eye...so it is, that this doctrine of the sacraments moves, stirs up and awakens most of the outward senses..."[1]

Baptism and communion are symbols of welcome, and inclusion, and remind us of the covenant relationship (God's promise of relationship with humanity in love and mercy) that gives shape, texture and dynamic to our faith and the way we live out our faith. The sacraments are intimately related to the affirmation that God is able to act in the world. In baptism, God reaches out to claim us, incorporate us into God's covenant people, and to draw us out of death into life. In the Lord's Supper, the Holy Spirit reminds us of the constant presence of Jesus amongst us, through the tangible reminders of bread and wine, pointing to Christ's death and resurrection, his suffering and his saving.

Part of the Church's function is to enable people to experience the sacraments and enable these symbols to add another dimension to our reflections on what the gospel is about. Who is the God we worship? What does God think about us? What about the journey of faith and the people we encounter on the way? Sacraments are there partially to help us wonder about the meaning and shape of our faith. The sacraments point to the very heart of the Gospel.

The Church of Scotland recognises two sacraments, baptism and the Lord's Supper or communion. The administration of sacraments is a ministerial act, and the Kirk Session is not constituted prior to a baptism or the Lord's Supper. Elders play a part in encouraging parents to bring their children to baptism, or encouraging adults seeking baptism to come forward; and elders have traditionally played a role distributing the elements of bread and wine at Communion (though others can help distribute the elements too). It is the practice of the Church of Scotland that the administration of the sacraments should always be accompanied by the preaching of the Word.

Baptism is the point where an individual – infant or adult – is welcomed into the family of faith, the Church. In the case of children, parents or guardians make promises relating to their own faith, and promise to ensure that the baptised child will learn about the Christian faith and move towards making their own profession of faith. Baptisms are part of a Sunday service (with very few exceptions). The congregation present makes a promise to play its part in living out faith around all children and so bolster the child's experience of inclusion and welcome within the broader family of faith. For adult baptism, the adults make their own promises as they are welcomed into the Church community. Adult baptism is often accompanied by admission to communicant membership, or confirmation. At both infant and adult baptism, the Aaronic blessing is often sung by the congregation (Numbers 6.24)

Baptism is a gift from God to the individual, a blessing through the Holy Spirit, and the element of water is always associated with baptism. Clearly baptism involves the community of faith, and is a reminder to all Christians that the responsibility of welcome and inclusion, nurture and encouragement is something in which the whole family of faith shares. Elders, if involved with the pastoral ministry of a congregation, can play a role in ensuring that baptised children, and those who are baptised as adults, find ways into the life of a congregation.

The Lord's Supper is an act of remembering the love of God shown through the events of Jesus' crucifixion and resurrection. Communion is also an act of thanksgiving (the Greek word for thanksgiving is the root of the word 'Eucharist', another name for Communion). It is focussed on the event on the Thursday of Holy Week where Jesus gathered with his followers in an upper room in Jerusalem to participate in Jewish Passover ceremonies. As part of the meal, bread and wine were blessed, the bread broken and the wine shared, representing the breaking of Jesus' body and the spilling of his blood when he was crucified. The bread and the wine are given "for us", the elements being given as food for our spiritual life. A leading Reformer, John Calvin, wrote, "These benefits are to foster, refresh, strengthen and exhilarate." The words used to institute the Lord's Supper are taken from Paul's First Letter to the Corinthians (I Corinthians 11.23-26).

Communion engages us with the body of Christ, not only symbolically through sharing the bread and wine and remembering, but also through the passing of the elements one to another. Traditionally the role of the elder has been to take the bread and the wine to the people, variously seated at tables, in pews, or standing in a circle around the communion table. Communion is, in many ways, a totally corporate activity. It engages the family of faith in the act of remembering and thanksgiving. Jesus is present with us always but Christians have argued that there is a focus, a special intensity at communion where the presence of Jesus appears amplified and more vivid.

Eating together is an intimate act. The practice of hospitality – of giving and receiving – is intrinsic to our Christian faith. The Lord's Prayer asks for daily bread. Jesus continually shared meals with people, and drew no distinctions between fellow diners. All were welcome then, and remain welcome now. Here is an image not only for communion but for all of our table of fellowship and church activity. It shows us something about God's Kingdom, where places at the table are set, and everyone is invited to eat and drink. We are called to live in this radical way, to bear witness to Christ's welcome that we ourselves experience.

When thinking about these essentials of faith, Robert Bruce, in 1589, perhaps sums up best when he concludes that we are invited to listen to the Word, and serve the Sacraments, "that you may begin your heaven here".[2] ■

Questions for discussion

1. What are you meant to think, feel and believe when participating in the Sacraments?
2. How does your church make baptism feel like an action of welcome and inclusion?
3. How does your church make the Lord's Supper a meal of remembering and thanksgiving?

Further reading

- Duncan B. Forrester and Doug Gay (eds.), **Worship and Liturgy in Context** (London, SCM Press, 2009)
- Donald K. McKim, **Introducing the Reformed Faith** (Louisville: Westminster John Knox Press, 2001).
- William Barclay, **Beginner's Guide to the New Testament** (Edinburgh: Saint Andrew Press, 2007).

Why not try... providing resources to help parents with newly baptised infants, or adults recently baptised, to explore the Christian faith?

Also, try exploring different liturgies and practices at communion services.

1. John Laidlaw (ed.), *Robert Bruce's Sermons on the Sacrament: done into English with a biographical introduction* (Edinburgh: Oliphant, Anderson & Ferrier, 1901), pp.1-2.
2. John Laidlaw, *Robert Bruce's Sermons on the Sacrament*, p.218.

CREATING COMMUNITIES OF BELONGING

John Swinton
Professor of Practical Theology and Pastoral Care,
University of Aberdeen

In this short article I want to offer elders a way of looking at being with people who have disabilities which is respectful, faithful and true to the Gospel that we seek to proclaim. The apostle Paul tells us that we are all part of the one Body of Christ. We are so deeply intertwined that what happens to one part of the body affects all of the body (1 Corinthians 12). More than that, those parts of the body that the world considers to be weak and undesirable are in fact vital for the whole of the body. One of the tragedies of our society (and, sadly, often our Churches) is the fact that many assume that people with disabilities are weak or "undesirable". Paul indicates strongly that there is no place for such attitudes in God's Church. As elders it is our responsibility to ensure that the Body of Christ is not broken by exclusion. In what follows I will suggest that if we cannot effectively include people with disabilities, we will have a hard time claiming that we are really the Church. Paul's vision in Galatians 3.28 of a community within which there is "No longer Jew or Greek, there is no longer slave or free, there is no longer male and female", can easily be extended to breaking down the barriers between black and white and able-bodied or disabled. Within the community of the Church, differences can never be barriers. God has no favourites (Romans 2.11).

Included but not belonging

Let me begin with a story. A few years ago I spent some time with Elaine, a middle-aged woman with a disability. She told me how hard it was for her to find friendships. She was very lonely sometimes. Elaine loved going to chapel and attended regularly. She participated in the worship and loved having tea with her friends after the service. But then I asked her how often she saw her church friends during the week? "Never," she replied. Within the boundaries of the religious service of worship she seemed to have found acceptance and a certain level of friendship. However, that acceptance and friendship stopped at the door of the chapel. She effectively had a friendship that lasted for an hour and a half on a Sunday morning. Elaine was included within the fellowship of the church, but she did not belong.

In the room but not of the room

Kieran's story is similar. Kieran is a young man who has a significant learning disability. He is confined to a wheelchair and has limited speech. But he loves to go to church. Well he used to. Kieran lives in a care home. His carers had decided that it might be a good thing to take Kieran to church. They knew that he loved to sing and to listen to music and he had been quite involved with a church when he was younger. So they took him to the local church. During the three months he attended, not one person spoke to him. One person patted him on the head in passing but that was it! The staff wondered if people were scared of Kieran, or embarrassed, or uncertain how to approach him. Either way, the experience was not a good one and they decided there was little point in Kieran continuing to attend. One member of staff said: "Kieran gets a more positive response in the local coffee shop". Kieran has not been involved in any faith community since. He was in the church but not of the church; he was included, but he did not belong.

THE TASK OF CHURCH LEADERS IS TO CREATE THE CIRCUMSTANCES WHERE COMMUNITIES OF BELONGING BECOME A GENUINE POSSIBILITY.

Beyond inclusion to belonging

The problem with a focus on including people with disabilities in our church communities is that, to include someone, they simply have to be in the room. All you need is access: ramps, large-print hymn books, hearing loops etc. As long as people with disabilities are in the room they are, at least in principle, included. Politics, disability legislation and human rights may well be necessary for people with disabilities to gain access to our communities, but they can never be enough. The Church is required to move beyond mere inclusion to belonging.

As Jean Vanier and I have said, Jesus' friendships urge us to move beyond inclusion towards belonging. To belong, you need to be missed: people need to miss you and to long for you when you are not there. To belong we need to feel that we matter. Belonging is the place where we truly meet. The Body of Christ is only truly the Body of Christ when all peoples have a place where they belong. The heart of the Gospel is all about belonging and this destroys fear and loneliness. It compels us to renew our minds and change our hearts.[1]

The task of Church leaders is to create the circumstances where communities of belonging become a genuine possibility. If people with disabilities are not amongst "us" or feel that they cannot be with the Church, then the Church really cannot be "the Church".

Guiding people towards the formation of this kind of community does not mean creating new programmes or developing specialist disability ministries. Such things might be useful, but unless our hearts are changed nothing will change. All of us (able bodied and disabled), need to have our minds renewed (Romans 12.2) in order that we learn what it means to live together as one Body in Jesus. The task for

leadership is twofold. Firstly, to help people to notice the subtle (and not so subtle!) ways in which people with disabilities are prevented from finding places of belonging within our Churches. This simply means noticing experiences such as Elaine's and Kieran's and mobilising others to notice and to act differently. Of course we can't force people to be friends with others, but we can create a situation where offering friendship is the norm.

Secondly, leaders need to encourage people to offer and to receive hospitality. Often when it comes to being with people living with disabilities the tendency is to want to be hospitable towards them. That is fair enough. However, hospitality is a two-way street. When you look at the life of Jesus it is clear that he was sometimes a guest and sometimes the host. The constant movement from guest to host is a mark of divine hospitality. What might it look like to us if we perceived ourselves as guests before people with advanced dementia? What if we thought of ourselves as guests in the lives of people with mobility impairments or people with learning disabilities – guests who are there to learn and not to teach, guests who are open to the gifts that emerge from being with people whose lives are lived differently. When we learn to live in such ways we become hospitable people who long to create hospitable spaces where people truly belong.

Friendship, belonging, noticing, guesting and hosting: these are not complicated gifts to offer to one another. But in their simplicity we will encounter Jesus and, as we encounter Jesus, we can truly become a Church within which there is neither Jew nor Gentile, neither slave nor free, male nor female, able-bodied nor disabled, only people who belong together in Jesus. ∎

 Questions for discussion

1. Is it fair to say that the Church cannot really be the church without the presence of people with disabilities?
2. What might be the main things that need to be done if your church is to become a community of belonging?
3. In what ways does being a "guest" move us beyond "inclusion" to "belonging"?

 Further reading

- Roy McCloughry, **The Enabled Life: Christianity in a disabling world**, (London: SPCK Publishing, 2013)
- Jean Vanier and John Swinton, **Mental Health: the inclusive church resource**, (London: Darton Longman and Todd, 2014)
- Gordon Temple, **Enabling Church: a Bible-based resource towards the full inclusion of disabled people**, (London: SPCK Publishing, 2013)
- Find out more at: **www.churchofscotland.org.uk/learn**

 Why not try... to organise an event when the congregation can come together to talk about disability issues and how they relate to their faith?

KIRK SESSIONS: LISTENING AND ACTING

Anne Law

Elder at Linlithgow: St Michael's Church, Presbytery of West Lothian

The Kirk Session is a court of the Church of Scotland and not just another committee of a club. For me that means that we should deal with each other in a distinctive way: always with love, courtesy and care. There should be opportunities to discuss issues productively and positively and the opportunity to challenge stances – but how can we do that in a positive way? I think that we manage challenge and criticism better in the workplace than in this court of the Church, and again I wonder how that can possibly be the case. Are we more likely to accede to others' views at work because there is a recognised hierarchy and authoritative specialists in the workplace whereas we sense that we have greater opportunity to influence in a Kirk Session, and perhaps get our own way?

I think that, particularly in larger Kirk Sessions, it is important that we get to know each other and develop relationships with each other for the sake of the 'unity and peace of this Church' as referenced in the affirmation of the elder at ordination. If we understand each other better we know where we are coming from. We learn where there are pockets of expertise and knowledge. We will also learn when others have issues or worries which are causing them concern. We might even have some fun together!

Kirk Session meetings will always begin with a short act of worship and it is that act of worship which sets the meeting apart from any other meeting that we might attend. We are united in Christ and, as it says in 2 Corinthians 5, "From first to last, this has been the work of God". We come together to do the work of God in our congregations and parishes.

I know of some Kirk Sessions where they will have a "check-in" time with each other at the start. The moderator allows five minutes at the start for elders to go into small groups and get to know each other better. This provides elders with the opportunity to share any issues that have arisen. Sitting round small tables rather than in rows might help to promote getting to know each other better – it is so simple and yet what a change that can bring.

You might like to consider developing teams within your Kirk Session to provide support for each other. In my own Kirk Session we have created support teams for elders by grouping district elders together. We meet three times each year so it is not an onerous commitment. We talk confidentially about any issues we might be having in our districts and also have another focus each time we meet. That could be a speaker – for example, we might hear from our youth worker, or discuss a particular topic together. I now have a great group of elders that I know that I can contact for assistance or support.

The operational work of a Kirk Session is usually carried out through its committee or task group structure, or the Congregational Board. It does no harm to review the make-up of each of these groups to ensure that the best use is being made of the talents of those involved. Just as it cannot be assumed that every elder is called to a pastoral role and district visits, there may be members of the congregation who have skills/gifts to bring to the Kirk Session committees or Congregational Board and who could be co-opted on to a committee in order to ensure that their skills and gifts are utilised.

At a workshop I ran called 'Making Meetings Effective' we considered the different kinds of folk that we are as we come to the Kirk Session meetings. Here are some highlights:

1. Some of us like time to reflect and find it difficult to speak out.
2. Some of us make too much noise and don't listen enough.
3. Some of us prefer to have conversations with the folk beside us rather than to address the meeting.
4. Some of us use our influence outside of the Kirk Session (in one of the famous car park meetings!).
5. Some of us can be stubborn.
6. Some of us want peace and harmony above all else and will try to keep everyone happy, but end up pleasing no one.

How would you suggest that we cope with the various behaviours listed above and get the best out of people? I have noted below some of the recommendations that I have received at the meetings workshops:

a. For those who like to reflect and find it difficult to speak out, papers for meetings have to be sent out in advance.
b. Elders can provide feedback to the clerk before the meeting.
c. The role of the moderator is crucial in ensuring that the more voluble members of Session do not have all the air-time; set a time limit to all speakers if needs be.
d. Discussion, perhaps outside of the Kirk Session meeting, will help to show why a colleague feels so strongly about an issue. Sometimes our stubbornness might mask a lack of confidence, say in our ability to change.
e. We might try to close down discussions too soon as we want to avoid any discussion which we view as an argument. Colleagues with this approach will need reassurance about their value and their contribution. ∎

Questions for discussion

1. How can we get to know and understand the individuals within our Kirk Session better?
2. How can we interact with each other more effectively and disagree more positively?
3. How can we become a more caring Kirk Session?

Why not try... some social endings to Kirk Session meetings – for example at Christmas?

Also, try starting your Kirk Session meetings with some catch-up time with each other.

PEACE AND UNITY OF THE CHURCH

Hugh Donald

Place for Hope, www.placeforhope.org.uk

Three short articles on Peace and Unity of the Church.

Article 1:
Why is peace and unity challenging?

The affirmation of the elder at ordination in the Church of Scotland includes the promise to "seek the unity and peace of this Church." These words may be easy to affirm. However, in the heat of the moment, faced with that difficult person or risk of losing a long valued tradition, all sense of seeking peace and unity so quickly evaporates. If we are honest with ourselves we have all had this experience and being a Christian does not stop us from being human. At the same time unity does not mean uniformity. Unity needs to embrace difference and diversity.

Through Place for Hope, we have had the privilege of working alongside Kirk Sessions in times of change, in times of conflict and in times of seeking new ways of relating to one another. Place for Hope, with its roots in the Church of Scotland, supports and equips churches to develop creative, positive and life-giving ways to explore and address differences, shaping a culture that acknowledges differences and demonstrates diversity in love.

Drawing upon this experience, let us explore three questions:

· Why is seeking peace and unity challenging?
· What are some of the skills needed to develop peace and unity?
· How can we learn to live a life in the ways of peace and unity?

It is intended this will offer some practical insights for all elders, regardless of length of service, as you individually and collectively seek the unity and peace of this Church.

Why is seeking peace and unity challenging?

As the words "peace and unity" trip off the tongue, it might be assumed that a gathering of elders is a group of like-minded people who all think very similarly and that a spirit of Christian love will automatically overrule all difference. The reality is that we are all different. We are unique in age, gender, sexuality, culture, personality, behaviour, and experience. We each have our own

unique story. God created each of us different. "I am fearfully and wonderfully made," says the psalmist at Psalm 139.14. These differences are our life-blood but at the same time a source of what can lead to a lack of peace and to disunity.

These differences extend to how each of us responds to disagreement and conflict. Some will readily embrace disagreement and others avoid it. Some will more readily seek to accommodate the needs of others. Some will always look for compromise or collaboration until a solution emerges. There is no right or wrong approach, rather a need to be aware of our own reactions and those of others.

The Kirk Session meeting is convened as a court of the Church of Scotland, seeking to address a wide range of issues – sometimes with very large numbers, sometimes very few. It is constantly encountering change, be it a new minister, a lengthy vacancy, a linkage or a union. Over time, such systems can prove clunky and unwieldy and a challenge in themselves to maintaining peace and unity.

Beyond all this, our churches sit within a fast-changing culture where church attendance on a Sunday is a far cry from the norm, raising critical questions around the Church's vision, mission and faith.

Seen in this context of all our individual differences, and the many societal pressures, it is understandable that seeking peace and unity is inevitably challenging and that we need to learn the ways of doing it well. A starting point is to accept that conflict is normal. It was a part of Jesus' ministry and reflected much of the life of the early Christian Church. Conflict can be a sign that people care. Conflict has the potential to hurt whilst at the same time to be a catalyst for transformation. The challenge is not the existence of conflict but rather how conflict is addressed. It may also be a time when we hear God's voice as we never have before. There is a need to discover the skills and the ways of embracing conflict healthily. This requires courage as we seek to become more aware of ourselves and others.

 Questions for discussion
1. Read Acts 15. What do we learn about how the early Christian Church addressed conflict ?
2. Conflict is presented as sometimes constructive. Can you think of examples? If conflict is destructive what makes it so?
3. Reflect upon a time that you have been in conflict. What responses did you have to the conflict? If you could revisit the situation, what might you do differently?

 Why not try... sharing your personal response to question 3 among others, perhaps the Kirk Session? You may find it helpful to evaluate your individual response to conflict situations with reference to the Thomas Kilmann conflict model www.kilmanndiagnostics.com

Article 2:
What are some of the skills needed to develop peace and unity?

We will all have experienced meetings where conflict arises through an inappropriate choice of words, an abrasive tone and what we experience as bullying behaviour. We may have experienced times when we have bottled up what we felt needed to be said, more comfortable to let off steam in the car park at end of the meeting. To seek peace and unity, there is a need to find the means to be open, honest, and respectful to each other. This is a lifelong journey; below are some key skills to consider.

Build relationships

At the heart of conflict is the mis-truth that somebody else is the problem. To address difference and diversity we need to get to know the other. Sadly many of our relationships in church are superficially reflected in the "How are you this morning?" together with the "I'm fine" response. Limited time is spent in Session meetings to learn more about each other. It is easy to relate to those with whom we agree, but less so to those with whom we disagree.

A good starting point for building peace and unity is to develop relationships. Once we are able to share our story and hear the stories of others around us, common ground can be found and our differences better understood.

Suspend assumptions

How quickly we can jump to assumptions. Whenever we meet someone for the first time we form value judgements within seconds and often without anything being said. Entering into a debate over the removal of the pews or a change in worship patterns can quickly become polarised due to assumptions being made, perhaps about why someone appears to be taking a particular stance or agreeing with a particular individual. Our churches are places where people are labelled, for example as conservative, liberal, traditionalist, modernist and so on. Labels mean we immediately categorise individuals. To build peace and unity we need to avoid the labels and to suspend our assumptions. Catch yourself when you are jumping to assume and hang that assumption from the ceiling!

Recognise differing perspectives

We naturally approach difference from our own perspective. That perspective is informed by our view of the issue, the facts we have available and our own insights. With that perspective, we quickly fall into the trap of assuming we are right and the other is wrong.

Yet the other has their perspective informed by their own understandings which they equally see as valid. For example, an elderly lady was sitting in a meeting in which several people were expounding an exhaustive list of complaints about the minister. Very quietly, and slightly tearfully, the lady shared her story of the minister: the minister had shown her great care and compassion. It did not invalidate the perspectives shared by the others but there was now another very different perspective to be embraced. To build peace and unity, there is a need to recognise that there are often multiple perspectives.

Compassionate listening

If there is only one skill to be exercised it has to be the skill of listening. How often in addressing a controversial subject at a Session meeting do we fail to really listen to what others are saying. We have closed down because we think we have heard the same old arguments many times before or are busily preparing our own arguments to respond. We want to jump in because our argument is better.

Listening involves some specific skills. It is important to listen to what is being communicated through all the words spoken, through all that is not said as well as through all the non-verbal expressions. It requires practice to listen to someone with whom you disagree or who is very different. It is listening in order to seek understanding not necessarily agreement. It is ensuring ways in which all voices are heard at Session meetings not just a few. Be brave, ask those around you if they felt heard and take to heart what they say.

As these skills are practiced and embraced, peace and unity becomes a way of being.

 Questions for discussion:

1. As we seek to listen to others, we also need to listen to God. How much time do you spend speaking to God and how much in listening? What might you do to enhance your listening to God?
2. In reflecting upon a difficult conversation you have had, what assumptions have you made about the other? How did those assumptions affect your ability to listen?
3. In what ways in your Kirk Session might you build deeper relationships?

 Why not try... scoring the effectiveness of your Kirk Session meetings out of 10? Consider different elements: decision-making, relationships, enabling different voices to be heard. What might you do to improve these scores?

Article 3:

How can we learn to live a life in the ways of peace and unity?

How can we learn to live a life in the ways of peace and unity? This is the challenge: to learn to walk a life of peace and unity.

Our calling is to a ministry of reconciliation. We are called to shape our lives, and that of the Church and society around us, in accordance with being reconciled with God. Being reconciled with God provides the energy and impetus to be reconciled with others.

All this is from God, who reconciled us to himself through Christ, and has given us the ministry of reconciliation; that is, in Christ God was reconciling the world to himself, not counting their trespasses against them, and entrusting the message of reconciliation to us.

2 Corinthians 5.18-19

This calling reflects a deep desire to repair broken relationships, to find a place of healing and a pathway to restored relationships and wholeness. It requires us to daily put on the new clothes described in Colossians 3 of compassion, kindness, humility, gentleness and patience.

To be reconcilers, we need to embrace the ways of forgiveness. Offering forgiveness is in our control – it is a choice we make independently of others. It is a way of releasing ourselves from the past, from the judgement of others and from our judgement of ourselves. It does not mean you agree with the other; it does not mean you can change what has happened. Martin Luther King describes it this way: "We must develop and maintain the capacity to forgive. He who is devoid of the power to forgive is devoid of the power to love. There is some good in the worst of us and some evil in the best of us. Forgiveness is not an occasional act. It is a permanent attitude."

Reconciliation is a language we have heard of in South Africa and in Northern Ireland. It is passionately desired in many parts of our world where conflict prevails. It is, however, just as relevant in our own lives, in our families, our Churches and our communities, where we are surrounded by broken relationships and a need for healing and forgiveness.

Some examples closer to home:

· How common it is to hear of broken relationships within the church, of two people, two families who have fallen out with each other often years ago and no one now really knows why. Is this to be perpetuated as a circle of rejection and revenge or is there the opportunity to choose healing? Desmond Tutu and his daughter Mpho Tutu talk of the forgiveness cycle in which the opportunity is taken to break out of the circle of revenge and to name the hurt, granting forgiveness and renewing or releasing the relationship. It takes courage to take the first step, and at the same time it opens the door to hope.

· Linkages and unions of churches are increasingly more common. They bring with them fresh challenges and opportunities. However, they can cause resentment, uncertainty and lack of trust. It is a time of loss which is often not recognised. We can become trapped in the past. A pathway to reconciliation recognises and celebrates the past, grieves the loss, forgives the misguided words or actions and seeks to build trust.

· Our Churches are faced with a range of difficult issues to address which can be divisive and result in broken relationships individually and collectively. Human sexuality is one such issue. A pathway to reconciliation faces up to these difficult issues and explores the ways in which individuals are respected whatever different opinions are voiced, where the process is not that of debate but of dialogue, not right or wrong, but listening to seek understanding rather than agreement.

Echoing the words of Colossians 3.14, we are called to bear with each other and forgive whatever grievances we have against one another. "And over all these virtues put on love, which binds them all together in perfect unity. Let the peace of Christ rule in your hearts, since as members of one body you are called to peace. And be thankful."

May this be the pathway we all seek to walk. ■

Questions for discussion

1. Reflect upon Colossians 3. What does it say to you about walking in the ways of peace and unity?
2. What is meant by forgiveness and why do we find it difficult?
3. Is there someone with whom you need to be reconciled? What do you need to do to take the first step?

Further reading

- Brian Castle, **Reconciliation: the journey of a lifetime**, (London: SPCK, 2014)
- Emmanuel Katongole and Chris Rice, **Reconciling All Things**, (Illinois: IVP, 2008)
- Desmond Tutu and Mpho Tutu, **The Book of Forgiving**, (London: William Collins, 2014)
- Andrew White, **Father Forgive**, (Oxford: Monarch, 2013).
- William Barclay, **Insights Forgiveness: what the Bible tells us about forgiveness**, (Edinburgh: Saint Andrew Press, 2011).

Why not try... finding out more about the issues raised in these articles and exploring ways of being better equipped in the ways of peace and unity?

Contact us

Place for Hope
Email: contact@placeforhope.org.uk
Tel: 0131 240 2258
www.placeforhope.org.uk

" Above all, clothe yourselves with love, which binds everything together in perfect harmony.

PASTORING THE PARISH

Sheila Rae

Pastoral Care Team Convenor at Linlithgow: St Michael's Church, Presbytery of West Lothian

Pastoral care has often been the remit of the parish minister solely, but emerging figures from the Church of Scotland indicate that, within the next 20 years, there will be a serious shortage of ordained ministers. Given this concerning trend, while continuing to affirm the role of the parish minister within pastoral care, it seems timely to reconsider how the eldership can play their part in caring for the parish. Indeed, pastoral care should be seen as a responsibility of the Kirk Session.

Often, elders are assigned districts to provide pastoral oversight, but just because someone is a district elder does not necessarily mean that they have the necessary skills or desire to make effective visits. The particular gifting of an elder may lie in a different area, but caring for our communities is our Christian calling. In Acts 20.28 Paul says, "Keep watch over yourselves and over all the flock, of which the Holy Spirit has made you overseers, to shepherd the church of God that he obtained with the blood of his own Son." In fact, a quick look through Scripture leaves no doubt as to what care the congregation has the right to expect: see, for example, 2 Corinthians 1.4 and Romans 12.4-21. A pastoral care team can help and support the district elder.

...BRING THE LOVE OF CHRIST INTO DIFFICULT SITUATIONS SO THAT THE QUALITY OF LIFE OF INDIVIDUALS IS IMPROVED...

Just what is pastoral care? This is an interesting exercise to do with the Kirk Session. Everyone thinks that he or she knows how to define it, but when put on the spot the answers are wide-ranging. It can be helpful to agree a definition of pastoral care for your own church and congregation.

The mission statement of St. Michael's Pastoral Care Team (PCT) is: to provide relevant, effective and accessible pastoral care and support services based on Christian commitment, insight and values and operating to the highest standard of ethics and practice for the members of St Michael's Parish Church, Linlithgow and also to non-members residing within the parish, irrespective of faith, cultural background, ethnic origin or life choices.

The PCT has a membership of 11 people, including our three ministers, the convenor and depute convenor. The other six people have been invited onto the team because of their special skills. This team is a business team, reporting and accountable to the Kirk Session and to the Ministry Team. It develops, implements and evaluates the pastoral care policies for the church, following agreement from the Kirk Session. The PCT also trains, develops and supports the church visitor team and the bereavement support team. It assists and supports the ministry team and eldership in the provision of pastoral care to the church congregation and to the parish. It has a responsibility to maintain an up-to-date pastoral visiting list, to assign church visitors and to organise home communions. The team sends out bereavement cards on the first anniversary of death and first anniversary

cards to those married in St Michael's, and organises the delivery of church flowers. The team also develops the prayer life of the church which includes Wednesday prayers and praying with people following the morning services.

The Protection of Vulnerable Adults legislation means that the work has increased for those involved in ensuring that all serving on the church visitors team are safeguarded, interviewed, trained and supported.

To ensure that the training of our church visitors and the members of the bereavement support team is effective, relevant and current, St Michael's have entered into a Memorandum of Understanding with Quiet Waters Charitable Trust. This is a Christian counselling, listening and training centre based in Falkirk. Our volunteers have been trained in active listening skills, in crisis management and in loss and bereavement. If a volunteer wishes to consolidate his or her skills they can become a Quiet Waters volunteer and shadow a trained listener. The bereavement team offers bereavement support both to individuals and to groups. They also assist the ministers with post-funeral visiting.

Our aim in providing such services is to bring the love of Christ into difficult situations so that the quality of life of individuals is improved by enhancing their ability to cope with their situation, be it sickness, bereavement, isolation or vulnerability.

Our core delivery of care is made up of visits from the ministers, district elders and church visitors, and the services provided by the bereavement support team and prayer team.

In conclusion, if pastoral care is the responsibility of Kirk Sessions, then it is incumbent upon them to think of fresh and innovative ways in which to deliver pastoral care. Be mindful that there is no "right" way of doing this but a good start might be to find people within the Session and congregation who are passionate about pastoral care. These people should have the right attitudes to caring and confidentiality and a willingness to develop and learn. Brainstorm the needs of the parish and see if there is any way in which they can be met. A starting point might be the forming of a coffee, cake and companionship group for the bereaved. Or is there a need to help young mums just home with a new baby. And what about hospital visiting or visiting the frail and lonely? The way in which pastoral care can be delivered is only limited by the extent of the collective imagination of the Kirk Session. ∎

Questions for discussion

1. In what ways can you develop pastoral care within your parish?
2. What skills and gifts do you think are needed to develop a pastoral care strategy?
3. What are the strengths with your current pastoral care provision? What areas require immediate attention?

Why not try... hosting a lunch for interested individuals within your congregation to discuss the pastoral care provision? Raise this at Kirk Session to ensure best support.

MAKING HOSPITAL VISITS

Blair Robertson

Head of Chaplaincy & Spiritual Care, NHS Greater Glasgow & Clyde.
Healthcare Chaplain, Southern General Hospital, Glasgow

'And when was it that we saw you sick or in prison and visited you?' And the king will answer them,
'Truly I tell you, just as you did it to one of the least of these who are members of my family, you did it to me.'

Matthew 25.39-40

The Gospels clearly show us that Jesus had compassion on those who were sick and suffering. The teaching of Jesus, in the Gospels, also reveals that he calls his followers to show compassion and care towards those who are sick. It is no mistake, therefore, that the Christian Church, and individual Christians, were among those who laid the foundations of modern hospital care and the hospice movement, among much else.

At any one time, there will be members of a congregation who are ill or injured and receiving medical care, at home, or in a hospital, hospice or nursing home. The pastoral care of the congregation ought to be extended to them and it is often the elder who will do that.

1. It's good to be remembered.

Mary has visited Alex in his nursing home for years but he has severe Alzheimer's and doesn't recognise her. She was feeling discouraged and asked the minister if there was any point in continuing to visit him. The minister replied, "We know that Alex gets very few visitors. I'd like to think that the church would remember him, even though he doesn't remember us. So, why not drop by every few months for a few minutes; leave the church magazine with him and make sure the staff know you've been. Let's show that he still matters to us."

The role of the elder

What is your role when you visit someone who is ill or injured? You might see yourself as their friend, and know that you will be welcomed as such. But you might not know them very well and be hesitant. In any case, if you are visiting in your role as an elder, you are a representative of the congregation and your visit has a dimension beyond a friendly, social call.

What can you do to make the visit – and the care - meaningful for both of you?

Do:
- visit with news of what's happening in the life of the congregation.
- take a recent congregational magazine or Order of Service to leave with the person.
- ask if there is anything else that you, or the congregation, can do to help.
- liaise with the relatives of the patient – they might appreciate your concern too or they might suggest that visiting would be better once the patient has returned home.

2. Permission to visit!

After Sunday worship, at the door of the church, Joe told the minister that Jean from his district was in hospital, and did she know?

"No, I didn't," she replied. "Have you visited her?"

"No," said Joe, a bit surprised.

"Tell you what," suggested the minister, "can you visit Jean and see how she's doing and let me know, please." In this way, Joe discovered he really had a role to play in the pastoral care of the congregation.

Confidentiality

The fact that someone is in hospital is their confidential business and it should not be shared with anyone without their permission. Similarly, if the person you are visiting mentions their diagnosis, or other personal matters, you cannot tell others unless the person has given you permission. You might want to ask if they want the minister to also know what they have told you.

Confidentiality is taken very seriously by medical staff and it is viewed as part of their duty of care towards a patient. This means that a nurse or a doctor will not be able to tell you about the patient's illness or treatment unless you have that right.

What do I do at the bedside?
Here are some simple Do's and Don't's for when you are visiting.

Do:
- call the ward (or a relative of the person) before you visit, if you can, to check the person is still there!
- find out when visiting times are.
- follow the infection control procedures in the ward – that might mean that flowers are not permitted.
- check with the patient that it's OK for you to visit: "is this a good time?"
- make sure that the patient knows who you are and will be able to remember you had been there!

Don't:
- visit if you have a cold or a bug – patients can be very prone to infections.
- sit on the bed or the chair next to the bed; there will be visitors' chairs for you to use.
- assume you have a right to be there, or outstay your welcome!
- make a bigger thing of the illness or injury than the patient is making of it.
- talk about your experiences of hospital or times you were unwell: the focus of your visit is the person you've come to see.

3. It's not always about listening.

John is in his early 80's and in an assessment ward for the elderly. He is quite forgetful and doesn't initiate conversations. He told a relative that he'd had a visit from his elder: "He was good. He talked about lots of things and I enjoyed his visit." Sometimes, patients appreciate news and a blether. Patients don't appreciate a visitor who sits in an embarrassed silence!

Healthcare Chaplains
Most NHS hospitals have a Healthcare Chaplaincy Service (or Spiritual Care Service.) The chaplain will be able to assist you with your visiting, if you feel you need it. Sometimes patients have to get medical treatment in a hospital a long way from home and it's hard for you or the minister to visit. The Chaplain in the hospital can be contacted to provide appropriate pastoral care. The phone numbers of Healthcare Chaplains for most NHS hospitals can be found in the Church of Scotland Year Book (every congregation should have one – check with your Session Clerk).

4. Some people enjoy hospitals.

Margaret had been in hospital over Christmas. When she got home she told her elder, "It was the best Christmas I'd ever had. I had nothing to do – no running around after anyone. The food was fine and the nurses made it as special a day as they could." ■

Questions for discussion

1. Read again the four stories about people in hospital. What do they suggest to you about the role of the elder?
2. What Bible readings might be appreciated by someone in hospital? And why? (For example, have a look at Psalm 63.)
3. Think about a time you were ill and in hospital (or at home.) Write down what was helpful at that time, and what was not helpful. Discuss your lists with others, if possible.

Further reading

- Philip Yancey, **Where is God when it hurts?**, (Michigan: Zondervan, 1997)
- Tom Gordon, **A Need for Living: Signposts on the Journey of Life and Beyond**, (Glasgow: Wild Goose Publications, 2007)
- Have a look at resources on the Methodist Church in Great Britain website
- **www.methodist.org.uk/ministers-and-office-holders/pastoral-care**

Why not try ... after visiting someone ill at home or in hospital, to write about the visit for five minutes? When you have finished, read over what you have written:
a. Circle the most important words for you in what you have written.
b. What did you learn from that visit?
c. Give your five–minute story a title that sums it up.
If you live close to a hospital, contact the Healthcare Chaplain there and ask if they can give you a tour of the hospital and an opportunity to ask questions about visiting people.

CARING FOR THE BEREAVED

Christopher Rowe

Minister of Colston Milton Parish Church,
Presbytery of Glasgow

" Do not be afraid to ask
how they are feeling.

I am a Church of Scotland minister within one of the Church's designated Priority Area parishes. I spend a lot of my time caring for the bereaved, especially in the conduct of funerals (about 30-40 a year), mostly those of folk I've never met before. Funerals are an important way that the church can help and care for people, but it is not the only way, and I hope it is not the only way your congregation cares for the bereaved. In this article I highlight different ways that elders and others, alongside the minister, could get involved in caring for those who have faced/experienced bereavement.

You can, of course, conduct a funeral – it is not the sole prerogative of the minister. Ask your Session Clerk or Presbytery for more information. There is also the task of ongoing care for the bereaved. Reflect on your own experience of grief to kindle your wish to care, aware that grief affects people differently.

Most of my funerals are held in the local crematorium; rarely is our place of worship used, even for members. I think to be able to offer and encourage the use of our places of worship for funerals is a huge gift we can give to our people, church-goers and not. Our places of worship are our spiritual homes, and they allow us to be gracious and hospitable towards our guests.

I am always impressed at local Roman Catholic funerals that they deeply involve neighbours and "well-kent faces". We have the opportunity to demonstrate love and concern by having people on hand to guide, read lessons, lead prayers and to play music – very much like a Sunday morning.

In preparing for a funeral I meet with the family, usually for about one to two hours. During this time together I ask lots of questions about the deceased, not just about the bare biographical details, but about the funny stories, the things they loved doing. It is always a helpful time for the family to remind themselves of who this person was, remembering, perhaps, not just the old lady who for the last months was bedridden, but recalling that she, too, was a young woman once, who loved and was loved.

In the funeral service, I spend about half the time telling the person's story, and afterwards it is amazing how people come and tell me "You got her just right". It is healthy and affirming to engage the bereaved in telling and retelling their memories and stories of their loved one; this is something all of us can do. Do not be afraid to ask people how they are feeling, and if you have a favourite memory of the deceased then tell their loved ones of it: they won't mind, but will be pleased that you also cared for them, and if they cry, don't be embarrassed for them or yourself.

If you are going to care for people through this difficult part of life you will need to be there: perhaps physically in their home, or on the phone or by letter, or even through text message or email.

Next stage: you have decided you want to visit the bereaved family and/or spouse but you feel a bit anxious, because perhaps they are a stranger to you. It is easier to knock on someone's door if you have an "excuse" or reason to be there: perhaps to drop off a card, or flowers, or some food (soup is always good!). Always have a calling card, so if they are not in you can let them know you came. Communicate that you have time to spend with them; don't just drop off the flowers and run away, but introduce yourself, say you are from the church, say you prayed for them on Sunday (if you did!); ask them how they are and whether there is anything you can do for them. You could even ask, "can I come in for five minutes?" Then sit with them, ask how they are coping, and don't be afraid to sit in silence. If you knew the deceased, tell the person you knew them, use their name, share a story – they will likely share their own stories too, and you should give time to listen to them.

If you were able to attend the funeral, it would be good to let them know that you were there and what being there meant to you; this communicates care and value. When you think it is time to go, offer to say a prayer with them. I strongly encourage you to try. It can be reading a prayer by you or someone else, or it could just come from the heart there and then. In your prayer it is helpful to reference elements of what you have discussed. This communicates care and compassion through careful listening, and demonstrates that their grief, worries and sadness have been brought before God. This can be a powerful experience for the bereaved person.

Often, at the point of prayer the person might begin to cry. Sometimes it is the space and privacy that they have needed to cry. Sit a while after you have said "Amen", with your eyes closed and head down – be sensitive to their need for time.

When you leave, give your contact details, and offer to come back. You can judge if they want to see you again or not. I usually only manage one visit, unless it is clear that the person would welcome ongoing care, but even if it is only one visit, or even a text message, people will know that someone cares. ■

ⓠ Questions for discussion

1. Talk about your own experiences of being bereaved – what hurt, what helped, how long did your grief last? What were for you the key markers of time – a week after the funeral, a month, a quarter, an anniversary, Christmas, birthdays?

2. How might you organise your care for the bereaved? It might include a rota of follow-up visits, responding to requests when they are made, sending flowers, praying in church for them, or writing letters or cards.

3. Generate a small list of ways in which you as elders could take a part to enhance a funeral service to show people that you care.

 Why not try ... on your next visit to a bereaved person having a prayer ready to say when you are with them?

HOW WILL OUR CHILDREN HAVE FAITH?

Suzi Farrant

Children and Young People Development Worker, Mission & Discipleship Council

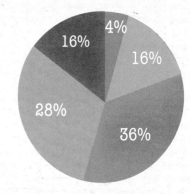

How will our children have faith? This is a burning question for Christian parents and Kirk Sessions as they consider how they are engaging with children and young people in the church. For some, the key concern might be: why are there no children and young people in our church?

The Church of Scotland annual statistical returns for 2012 showed over 65,000 children and young people (aged 17 and under) involved in the life of the Church – 14% of people in our congregations. Over 200 congregations reported no-one under 18 involved in their church, and a further 500 congregations reported under 20 young people in their church. This means that 52% of our congregations have fewer than twenty children or young people present.

Challenging statistics? Yes, but if we trust that God has a plan, this suggests that we have an opportunity.

What is the role of the Kirk Session? Each Kirk Session has a responsibility to implement church policy on education, provide access to training, appoint volunteers and implement the Church of Scotland's child protection policy.

Elders can meaningfully shape ministry with children and young people by taking a three-pronged approach:

a) Value children and young people as an integral part of the church community. Create the space within the Kirk Session's agenda to discuss this area of church life. Perhaps form a 'working group' to explore development opportunities.

b) Pursue a refreshed vision for ministry with children and young people. Perhaps read current thinking on ministry with children and young people – maybe start with the texts noted in Further Reading.

c) Invest in volunteers and paid workers who work with children and young people, seeking to support, develop and guide them. The national charter for church youth workers, 'We Love Our Youth Worker',[1] could be adapted to indicate seven values that a Kirk Session can adopt and develop to support their volunteers more effectively:

- Praying and supporting.
- Giving space for personal spiritual growth.
- Sharing responsibility.
- Delivering good management.
- Providing ongoing training and development.
- Celebrating and appreciating.
- Encouraging regular periods of rest.

Each Kirk Session will fulfil these promises in different ways according to their context so it is worth spending some time as a Kirk Session thinking through how to develop these principles. Perhaps it would be possible to invite volunteers to visit a Kirk Session meeting: this would allow them to report directly to the meeting but also to see the wider work of the church.

The opportunity is before us. Let's be active in hearing what the Spirit of God is saying about the role our congregations play in ministry with children and young people. ∎

1 For the full charter please visit www.weloveouryouthworker.org.uk

---

Under 18s in congregations

- No under 18s
- 1-20 under 18s
- 21-80 under 18s
- 81-199 under 18s
- 200+ under 18s

 ### Questions for discussion

1. What is the relationship between your Kirk Session and the children and young people in your congregation?
2. How can you help children and young people to play an active part in church life?

 ### Further Reading

- John H. Westerhoff III, **Will Our Children Have Faith?**, (New York: Morehouse Publishing, 3rd Revised edition, 2012)
- Ivy Beckwith and David Csinos, **Children's Ministry in the Way of Jesus**, (Illinois, IVP, 2013)
- Kara E. Powell, Brad M. Griffin, and Cheryl Crawford, **Sticky Faith Youth Worker Edition: practical ideas to nurture long-term faith in teenagers**, (Grand Rapids, Zondervan, 2011).

 Why not try... inviting the Youth Fellowship along to a Kirk Session meeting to tell you about what they have been doing and to hear any suggestions they may have?

DISCIPLESHIP

Neil Glover
Minister of Flemington Hallside Church, Presbytery of Glasgow; Ministries Council

When I think of "disciples" I imagine beards, sandals, men sitting on a hillside, fishing nets, multi-coloured striped dressing gowns, boats in storms. Perhaps something happened to me when I was at Sunday School in St. Vigean's, Arbroath in the 1970s. Someone must have said the word "disciple" and there must have been an illustrated Bible nearby. These were the images that filled the box in my brain marked out for "discipleship".

My reality is filled with running, working, fishing rods, freshly shaven face, and driving to where I need to get to. This seems a fair distance from my understanding of those first disciples. Somehow it feels like real disciples don't take a Saturday to mow the lawn, or reserve Tuesday evenings for committee meetings, or ever struggle to discipline their children (they appeared to have just left them while they went for a three-year walkabout).

Members of my congregation sometimes say to me "I'm not a real Christian because I don't ..." and then give a list of things they think they ought to be doing. They're doing the same thing as me with my beards and my fishing nets comparison. Discipleship seems "out there" – not something we do or can do in our own congregation. Let's look at discipleship a little more closely and check whether the items in our box marked "discipleship" do, in fact, include the things we do, and perhaps note some aspects we could take up.

Discipleship starts in an encounter with Christ in worship and prayer, and develops into a gutsy life that overflows with this living water. When I think of some of the folk in my congregation who inspire me most in discipleship, they are often the ones who enjoy worship, enjoy coming together as a congregation to pray and have a sense of "I was waiting all week for that".

Podiatry and Other Graft
I recently discovered that the Society of Chiropodists and Podiatrists is around the corner from our Church of Scotland central offices. This felt like a good reminder: that Jesus taught us, his Church, something profound in the washing of the disciples' feet.

Discipleship is not unrelenting chores, but can involve apparently menial tasks. A disciple is one who does the job some might think was beneath them for the benefit of their fellow human, like Jesus washing the feet of his disciples. He showed us something incredibly inspiring about discipleship: a love for one another that knows no bounds. I have seen this kind of love in the parish: for example someone caring for their husband or wife suffering from dementia. There is something exhausting, beautiful, relentless and raw about that, something that strips away all pretence to reveal bare humanity. Discipleship helps us become truly human and helps reveal the humanity of our fellow sisters and brothers.

 Discipleship is at the heart of our Christian life together: growth and transformation become the new normal...

Stand
Karl Martin is an influential pastor in Edinburgh and he is passionate about discipleship. He suggests that we are in a new age of Church life. This era sees a fresh energy in Church life for discipleship; this has the potential to bring incredible transformation to our congregations and communities. I find it telling that Karl's first book was not called "Walk" or "Follow" but "Stand".

The picture of 'standing' speaks to me about simply being, and being rooted in a way that we are thoroughly present: despite enormous pressure we remain fixed to our call. This is different from belligerent stubbornness. This is a commitment to the Christ we have encountered in worship - to be committed to a life of generosity and love.

This image of standing is seen in Matthew 7.24-27 when Jesus tells the story of a wise man who built his house on the rock. In Paul's great passage on spiritual armour in Ephesians 6, the primary instruction is to stand. Discipleship involves standing strong where you are, being rooted in Christ. The tree

Avid Hydrators and Watery Guts
Some people act as if discipleship is an endless desert marked by misery; right now we suffer but in heaven we will be rewarded. If you're having fun, then it probably isn't discipleship! Discipleship is a serious business of doing the jobs on the rota that no one else has signed up for. But this is not the picture that Jesus gives. In John 7.37-38 we hear Jesus describing discipleship like a drinking activity, which results in an overflow! "Come to me and drink!" says Jesus, and from the guts "will flow rivers of living water". Many translations say "heart" instead of "guts", but I prefer "guts" because it captures the fuller, less nice, more committed, aspects of discipleship: something that comes from the very centre of who we are.

stands strong because its roots go deep in the soil. We can stand strong as our lives become planted in Christ: this is the miracle of discipleship.

Discipleship, then, involves drinking, grafting and standing. We grow in discipleship by ensuring there is a balance of such things in our lives: we do intentional work on our diaries and our habits to ensure that we are not distracted and diverted. All of this is growth. This happens over a lifetime and through the miracle of the Holy Spirit.

How do we start this conversation in our Kirk Sessions? Through one of the most important documents: the agenda! Our meetings can be places when we consider how the church supports drinking (How is our worship?; How do we pray?), grafting (How do we serve?; How do we cherish our carers?), and standing (Where must we hold strong?; How deep are our roots?). This discussion works best with proper preparation, sufficient time, and clear subsequent action. Discipleship is at the heart of our Christian life together: growth and transformation become the new normal in this model. ∎

 Questions for discussion

1. Where are the sources of 'life-giving water' in your congregation?
2. In what ways can we better serve each other and our community as part of our life of discipleship together?
3. What are the key ways in which we grow as disciples?

 Further Reading

- Karl Martin, **Stand**, (Edinburgh: Muddy Pearl, 2013)
- John Ortberg, **The Life You've Always Wanted: spiritual disciplines for ordinary people**, (Grand Rapids: Zondervan Publishing, 2002)
- Henri Nouwen, **The Return Of The Prodigal Son**, (London: Darton, Longman & Todd Ltd., 1994).

Why not try... planning a conference or day retreat as a Kirk Session to explore discipleship?

MISSIONAL THINKING:
A LIGHT TO THE NATION

Alexander Forsyth
New College, University of Edinburgh

> " ...mission should be at the centre of the Christian life.

Since World War Two, the Christian Church globally has undergone a seismic shift in thinking about mission. This thinking is known as *missio Dei* (mission of God) theology. Rather than being an occasional function which belongs to the Church alone, mission is "God's activity, which embraces both the Church and world".[1] That realisation has very important consequences for everyone in the Church – not just the minister.[2]

Firstly, the Church can no longer be a triumphant institution ready to conquer the world around it, but instead it is being sent by God as part of God's mission in the world to further the kingdom. Mission is therefore to be carried out in a spirit of "bold humility".[3] Mission is exercised in "dialogue"[4] with others: listening not lecturing, being as much the learner as the teacher, our interaction forcing us to rethink our own understanding of the Gospel. There is also the necessary inclusion of the "prophetic", a sense of the presence of God in the encounter, whether in words or actions, which influences the direction of the journey thereafter.

Secondly, mission becomes a founding core of the Church, and so also of its lay people: mission is intrinsic to the Christian life. A focus on the mission of God being active in the world, in which we are invited to participate, changes the Church's perspective. Mission becomes the agenda, rather than an addendum to it. As God has called each of us within the Church to act to fulfil his purposes for humanity, mission should be at the centre of the Christian life.[5]

Thirdly, if this is so, the practical effect of the *missio Dei* is that the people of the Church are called to illuminate the Gospel in all that they say and do – to be a "light for the nation". But how is that to be done? In other words, what might "mission" be in your local context? The answer to that question defines the purpose of the Church.

Over the centuries, the parish system in the Church of Scotland became embedded in an "attractional" model, which was based on the assumption that Scotland was fully Christianised. The mere presence of the local church would be sufficient to bring those in the parish area within the church doors from duty and social habit. Mission happened abroad. There was thus little perceived need for the local church to devise any concept of what mission might entail on its own doorstep.

Those days have passed. What may be needed is not to do the old thing better, a "call to church" revival aimed at attracting people at the edges back into the building, but instead a movement towards an "encounter with the Gospel" in society, by the whole people of God to the whole of life around them.

The following definitions offered by the World Council of Churches of the breadth of such "mission", and its relationship to "evangelism", might provide one starting point for discussion:

a. "Mission" carries a holistic understanding of the proclamation and sharing of the good news of the Gospel by word (*kerygma*), deed (*diakonia*), prayer and worship (*leiturgia*), and the everyday witness of the Christian life (*martyria*); teaching as building up and strengthening people in their relationship with God and each other; and... reconciliation into *koinonia* - communion with God, communion with people, and communion with creation as a whole.

b. "Evangelism", while not excluding the different dimensions of mission, focuses on explicit and intentional voicing of the Gospel, including the invitation to personal conversion to a new life in Christ, and to discipleship.[6]

Another starting point for considering "mission" is to look towards six essential elements to which all concepts of mission ought to relate, no matter the theology: witness and proclamation; worship and prayer; seeking justice, peace and the integrity of creation; inter-faith dialogue; Gospel and its cultural context; and seeking reconciliation between people and with God.[7] Importantly, both salvation and social justice need to be addressed.

Rather than 'what should the Church do?', the key question for mission becomes 'how is Christ speaking now?' How is Christ speaking now in this time, in this place, to those who profess Christian faith, so as to engage with the people with whom they interact, in the society and culture in which they reside, in order that they might fully exercise in the world the work of God's mission, through the Word and Spirit of God? Mission is always contextual and no "one-size-fits-all" approach will sufficiently answer this key question. Every Christian community has to identify the relevant forms of mission for their particular context.

Everyone can exercise "mission" in their own small way. That focus may be the future of mission in today's increasingly secularised Scotland: in the slow, patient, organic growth of Christian communities by lay people, both within the pre-existing structures of the Church and outwith.

In the quarter-century after World War Two, across the Christian denominations in the Western World, there was a dramatic resurgence in the importance placed on the life and witness of ordinary people, expressing the Gospel in word and deed in ways that met the rhythms of everyday life. The Church of Scotland was at the forefront, through inspirational figures such as Tom Allan and George MacLeod. Is it not time to recapture their vision? ■

 Questions for discussion

1. What is "mission"?
2. In your context, how is Christ speaking in your time and place?
3. How can elders empower and inspire other members of the church to exercise their gifts in mission?

 Further reading

- Stephen Spencer, **SCM Study Guide to Christian Mission**, (London: SCM Press, 2007)

- David Bosch, **Transforming Mission: Paradigm Shifts in Theology of Mission** (New York: Orbis, 1991)

- Church of Scotland, **Who is my neighbour?: A user's guide to statistics for mission** (Available at www.resourcingmission.org.uk)

- Church of Scotland is a member of the World Council of Churches. Visit their website and search for *Together Towards Life:* **www.oikoumene.org**

 Why not try... identifying how "mission" could be exercised in different ways through the gifts of each member of your congregation; how can elders further encourage this?

1. Jürgen Moltmann, *The Church in the Power of the Spirit: a contribution to messianic ecclesiology* (London: SCM Press, 1977), p.64.
2. See Chapter 5 of the Church of England's *Mission-Shaped Church: Church Planting and Fresh Expressions of Church in a Changing Context* (London: Church House Publishing, 2004).
3. David Bosch, *Transforming Mission: Paradigm Shifts in Theology of Mission* (New York: Orbis, 1991), p.489.
4. See Stephen B. Bevans and Roger P. Schroeder, *Prophetic Dialogue: Reflections on Christian Mission Today* (Maryknoll, N.Y.: Orbis Books, 2011).
5. See Emilio Castro, 'Liberation, Development and Evangelism: Must We Choose Mission?', Occasional Bulletin for Missionary Research (July 1978), p.87, as quoted by Kirk, J. Andrew, *What is Mission: Theological Explorations* (London: Darton, Longman & Todd Ltd, 1999), p.31.
6. Mission and Evangelism in Unity Today (2000), para 7, within *You are the Light of the World: Statements on Mission by the World Council of Churches 1980-2005* (Geneva: World Council of Churches, 2005).
7. Bevans & Schroeder, *Prophetic Dialogue*, p.2.

ELDERS AND THE ENVIRONMENT

Adrian Shaw
Climate Change Officer,
Church and Society Council

Trevor Jamison
Environmental Chaplain,
Eco-Congregation Scotland

We believe that God made the universe, including this world, humankind and all the other flora and fauna with which we share this Earth. God also loves it; John's Gospel says that it was love for the world which led God to send Jesus into it (3.16). Since God loves the world, so should we.

God's love is expressed in action, not just words or feelings, and so our love ought to be displayed in action too. To love our neighbours leads us to take actions when they are adversely affected by things going on in God's world, and avoid actions which would harm others. Climate change brought about by burning of fossil fuels is now hurting our neighbours around the world and its impact will grow in years to come. This gives greater urgency to take actions we should be doing anyway: moved for and by the love of God.

The Church of Scotland is responding to climate change. Reports to General Assembly have called upon the Church of Scotland, its Presbyteries and congregations to take action; the Church has appointed a Climate Change Officer who seeks to encourage all congregations to become "eco-congregations". Over 200 Church of Scotland congregations have registered with Eco-Congregation Scotland, an ecumenical charity helping churches to link environmental issues to their Christian faith and encouraging them to take practical action in their church and community. Many congregations have subsequently received Eco-Congregation Awards to mark the work they have done in caring for the Earth, both in the church and in local communities.

Churches registered as eco-congregations have access to an Annual Gathering and 18 networks across Scotland, which meet to exchange information and ideas and take part in joint activities. They are supported by a field worker and an environmental chaplain (who is available to come to any church to speak, preach or lead worship). ∎

Questions for discussion

1. In what ways does your congregation currently include environmental topics in its worship and prayer, learning and teaching?
2. What actions have people you know taken in response to environmental concerns?
3. Are you aware of local community groups or organisations which have undertaken actions or projects to tackle climate change?

Further reading

- The Eco-Congregation website is a source of information and 'ideas for action'
  www.ecocongregationscotland.org
- The Church of Scotland works in partnership with Christian Aid to promote climate justice **www.christianaid.org.uk/ActNow/climate-justice**
- Church of Scotland information and resources
  www.churchofscotland.org.uk/speak_out/care_for_the_earth

Why not try ... registering your church with Eco-Congregation Scotland? Then appoint a small group to undertake the Eco-Congregation church check-up and to report back to Session. This will remind congregations what they already do to care for the Earth and provide pointers towards actions to do more. You can find out how to register at the Eco-Congregation website (noted above):

Contact us

Trevor Jamison
Environmental Chaplain,
Eco-Congregation Scotland
0131 225 5722
trevor@ecocongregationscotland.org

Adrian Shaw
Climate Change Officer
Church of Scotland
0131 240 2277
ashaw@cofscotland.org.uk

ECUMENICAL THINKING: WORKING WITH OTHERS

Theodora Hawksley

Post-doctoral Researcher, New College, University of Edinburgh

I would like you to visualise a room in your home. If you are at home at the moment, look up at the room you are in; if you are out or at work, picture a room in detail. What you are looking for is gifts. What items can you see that have been given to you? Who gave them to you? Was it an unexpected gift, something you would not have bought for yourself, but that you appreciated? Or was it something that you needed, or perhaps that you didn't realise you needed until it was given to you?

When we think about ecumenism, the words that come to mind are usually things like "dialogue" or "collaboration". Some ecumenical efforts have focussed on areas of theological disagreement and misunderstanding, and proceeded by way of bilateral and multilateral talks between denominations. These have been hugely important in addressing historical grievances and theological divisions, but the method has limitations.

The theological complexity of the agreements reached, and the small number of people involved in creating them, means that these talks sometimes have limited impact on the grassroots level. Moreover, there are some persistent differences of theology and practice that talks alone are unlikely to resolve. In addition to the dialogue approach, ecumenism has also progressed through practical collaboration across denominations, in which what

unites us – concern for social justice, or shared prayer - is in the foreground, and what divides us fades into the background. These, too, have been important in building relationships of respect and affection, but the collaborative approach also has its limitations: in focussing on what unites us, we can end up ignoring altogether what divides us and, for all its value and richness, the experience may not produce much institutional change.

Amid claims that we are living through an 'ecumenical winter', recent years have seen some in the ecumenical movement take up another image and method, alongside dialogue and collaboration: the image of gift, or a gift-exchange. If this exchange is to be possible, then we should move away from what we must teach to what we can learn. What we can share rather than how we can make "them" the same as "us".[1]

This approach to ecumenism arises from both pragmatic insight and theological conviction. Pragmatically, the receptive ecumenism approach recognises that full unity of doctrine and practice between Christian denominations is unlikely in the short-to-medium term, and therefore may not be the most helpful goal on which to focus our ecumenical efforts. Theologically, it springs from a belief that the unity we are called to seek is a unity-in-difference patterned after the life of the Trinity. Growing towards that unity-in-difference

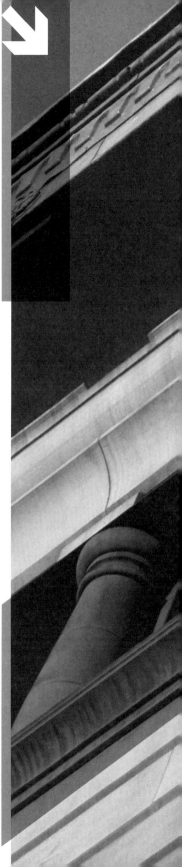

requires each church to pursue its own conversion, and the deepening and strengthening of its own faithfulness, mission and identity. Where this journey of conversion is undertaken in humble and generous conversation with ecumenical others, the hope is that it will result not in the entrenchment and the hardening of denominational boundaries, but in our growing together under the guidance of the Spirit who leads the whole Church into the fullness of the truth. Hand in hand with this theological conviction is the pragmatic conviction that, if all Churches shifted towards this way of thinking about and practicing ecumenism, we might find ourselves growing together in mutually enriching and perhaps surprising ways.

Ecumenical encounters can proceed on the basis that our denominational differences are not inherently problematic, to be eliminated where we can do so, or worked around where we cannot. The distinctive identities of the Churches can be sources of division, but they can also be gifts intended for the growth and upbuilding of the Church as a whole. Ecumenism can therefore take the form of a gift-exchange, in which we seek to receive things that we need from others, and in which we give things that others need or desire from us. Like any gift-exchange within a family or between friends, this demands that we know ourselves and our ecumenical others well. We will need to learn how to examine our own tradition, as well as the traditions of others, with the gaze of Christ as he looks at the rich young man (Mk 10.17–22): a look full of appreciative love, but able to discern what is lacking. We will need to be open to learning how others see us and rediscovering, through their eyes, our distinctive ecclesial gifts. And we will need to reflect on how, with integrity and humility, we can receive gifts from others that help us to grow in both faithfulness and unity. ■

 ## Questions for discussion

This kind of gift-exchange thinking is something you can do on a local level, as well as on a general or denomination-wide level.

1. Who are your local ecumenical neighbours?
2. Thinking prayerfully about your own local church, what gifts could you receive from your neighbours?
3. What are the gifts of your local church, and how could you share them?

 ## Further reading

- A list of resources and articles about the theology and practice of receptive ecumenism can be found on the website of the Durham Centre for Catholic Studies: **www.dur.ac.uk/theology.religion/ccs/projects/receptiveecumenism/publications**
- Paul D. Murray and Andrea L. Murray, **'The Roots, Range, and Reach of Receptive Ecumenism'**, in Clive Barrett (ed.), Unity in Process: Reflections on Receptive Ecumenism (London: Darton, Longman & Todd, 2012), pp.79-94.

Why not try... spending some time reflecting on how your ecumenical neighbours could help your own local church grow in faithfulness to its mission?

Read more about ecumenism on the Church of Scotland website:
www.churchofscotland.org.uk/connect/ecumenism

1 See Paul D. Murray, 'Receptive Ecumenism and Ecclesial Learning: Receiving Gifts for Our Needs', Louvain Studies (pp.30-45) p.32.

CENTRAL SUPPORT

Pauline Weibye
Secretary to the Council of Assembly

The Church of Scotland offices, famously based at 121 George Street in Edinburgh although with a few small offices in other parts of the country too, exist to support and serve congregations and Presbyteries. The marble halls can look daunting but it is the people within the offices who matter and they are the ones who can help elders, other office-bearers and members with any questions that arise – and I mean any questions, however simple or complex.

I became an elder 25 years ago and have been a Session Clerk for the last few years. I wish I had known years ago that so much support was freely available from the Church offices. We have around 200 staff to provide professional support to the 400,000 members, elders and ministers of our denomination. Some of our people work to keep the operations of the Church of Scotland functioning smoothly, for example supporting the recruitment and training of ministers, paying them their stipends monthly (and pensions, when they retire), assisting with ministers' retirement housing, processing safeguarding forms, engaging and supporting overseas mission partners, organising the General Assembly and providing resources and support for the Guild.

> **The marble halls can look daunting but it is the people within the offices who matter...**

We have experts who are only too willing to give you and your fellow elders the benefit of their knowledge and years of experience in the Church of Scotland. Does your congregation need legal advice about a property or staffing matter? Get it free from the Law Department, the staff of which have, between them, decades of experience of advising congregations and also offer very favourable estate agency and conveyancing rates if you are selling or buying a property. Or do you need help with a buildings problem? The General Trustees are here, ready to advise and assist, and sometimes even to provide financial support.

The Safeguarding Department employs professionally qualified social workers and also has personnel who used to work for the police; you can trust their advice if your congregation develops a safeguarding problem. And talking of problems, do you have the media camped on your doorstep? Don't panic,

call the Communications Department on its 24-hour helpline and we'll send someone to you to help if we can. Your Session Clerk and Minister probably have the Principal Clerk on speed-dial already; he and his department are always happy to advise and support congregations on matters of Church of Scotland law.

If you do not already have the Church website as one of your favourites, I suggest that you sort that – and then spend a happy couple of hours browsing the website and checking out the resources that are available for you to use. Look at the Resourcing Worship pages and get ideas for leading worship, making free use of the prayers, children's addresses and music suggestions that are updated weekly.

Check out the publications that you can order and use in your congregation: newsletters and leaflets from CrossReach, World Mission, Mission and Discipleship and Ecumenical Relations; guidance notes from the Law Department on data protection, food hygiene and the employment of local staff; information on stained glass, the disposal of redundant communion vessels, and disabled access to church buildings; and detailed statistical information on your parish and community. All are available for your use. (And do feel free to suggest other topics that we might not have identified ourselves.)

Most of the staff in the Church offices are, themselves, members of the Church of Scotland; some are elders and all are committed to giving you the information and support you need to help you fulfil the affirmation of eldership you made at ordination. We look forward to hearing from you. ∎

www.churchofscotland.org.uk